How to prepare for

IELTS

New edition

by
Ray de Witt

The British Council

About the author

Ray de Witt has taught English for specific purposes and English for academic purposes at the University of Westminster and Middlesex University. Since 1991 he has run an IELTS preparation course at the University of Westminster, where he had been an IELTS examiner since 1989. He has run successful IELTS teacher training seminars in Nicosia, Limassol, Belgrade and Skopje. He is the co-author of *Applied English, A teacher's manual on English for academic purposes*, published by the Open Learning Foundation. Ray de Witt is currently running Trinity Cert. TESOL teacher training courses in north London.

Author's acknowledgements

I should like to acknowledge the support and encouragement of John Hooton, Director of Short Courses at the former Polytechnic of Central London, in the setting up of my IELTS preparation course. This led directly to the production of materials which in turn have resulted in the publication of the first edition of this book. The exercises are mine, for which I accept full responsibility. Full credit must be given to the editor, Richard Law, for the book itself. He asks the impossible – and then makes quite sure he gets it!

I should like also to acknowledge the generosity of those students who gave their time in producing written work and in being interviewed. The format of these materials would, literally, not have been possible without their efforts. Thanks also to Rosa for trialling the first draft, to Eileen Lockwood for suggestions and support, and to Chiara Guida for help with manuscript preparation.

I would also like to thank Louisa Zavallis for her inspiration and determination in producing the section two practice materials for use in Cyprus.

I should also like to acknowledge the generosity of the copyright holders in giving permission to reproduce the extracts used for the reading passages.

Alison Martin had the deeply frustrating and largely thankless task of locating, contacting and chasing up copyright holders, which she undertook without ever once losing her smile. Thanks, Ali.

Last, but most important, thanks are due to the Design, Production and Publishing Department at the British Council for putting it all together.

All of the above would of course be irrelevant without IELTS and those who use it. If you are about to be an IELTS candidate, I hope the exercises will prove to be useful and I wish you well in the test itself.

To Fergus

Publisher's acknowledgements

The articles *How the brain reorganizes itself* and *Hidden history: the beetle's secret cycle of life* on pp. 13 and 10–11, together with figure 1, are reproduced from the *New Scientist*, volume 131, number 1776, 6 July 1991, pp. 15 and 43 respectively, with the permission of IPC. The article *Desktop publishing* on pp. 21–2 is reproduced from INFO, the official journal of the French Chamber of Commerce in Great Britain, volume 12, number 6, October 1990, with the permission of the French Chamber of Commerce in Great Britain. The articles *Recruitment trends across the Channel* and *Hi-tech connections* on pp. 28–9 and 18 are adapted from INFO, volume 14, number 2, March/April 1992, with the permission of the French Chamber of Commerce in Great Britain. The article *Perchance to dream* on pp. 19–20, together with figure 2, is adapted from *The mind machine* by Colin Blakemore published by BBC Books, with the permission of BBC Worldwide Ltd. The article *Social and cultural impacts of tourism in Cyprus* on pp. 15–16 was first published in *Tourism management*, volume 12, number 1, March 1991, and is reproduced here with the permission of Professor Stephen Witt and Butterworth-Heinemann, Oxford, UK. Many of the ideas in the article *Reading skills* on pp. 23–5 come from Tony Buzan *Use your head*, BBC, 1989. The article *Job satisfaction and personnel mobility* on pp. 63–4 is adapted from *The Sunday Times*, 1 August 1993, and is reproduced here with the permission of the author, Philip Schofield. The articles *The education gap*, *The urban revolution* and *Industrialization and development* on pp. 66–7, pp. 91–2 and pp. 97–8 respectively are adapted extracts from *WWF atlas of the environment*, Lean and Hinrichsen, Helicon, 1992. The articles *Developing environmental management strategies* and *Problems with contaminated land in the UK* on pp. 69–70 and pp. 103–4 respectively were first published in INFO, volume 14, number 6, October/November 1992, and are reproduced here with the permission of the French Chamber of Commerce in Great Britain. The article *Birth of a profession* on pp. 75–6 was first published in *CA Magazine*, October 1993. The article *Rethinking Europe: ICI and the Single European Market* on pp. 78–9 is adapted from the *Financial Times*, 1 February 1993. The articles *The Muddle of MBAs* and *Handling the high flyers* on pp. 81–2 and pp. 100–2 respectively, are adapted from *Management Today*, June and July 1993. The article *NVQs in retailing – the BHS experience* on pp. 85–7 was first published in the *NVQ Monitor*, June 1993, and is reproduced here with the permission of the author, Stephen Barber. The article *Harmful publications* on pp. 88–9 was first published in *Arts Education*, summer/autumn 1993.

Acknowledgement is given to the following for the use of statistical information: Antonis Andronicou, LL.B., Ph.D., formerly Director-General of the Cyprus Tourism Organization, table 1; Cyprus Ministry of Finance, tables 2 and 4 and figure 10; *The state of the world's children*, 1989 and 1991, United Nations Children's Fund (UNICEF), figures 6 and 11; Brodies Solicitors, figure 7; *WWF atlas of the environment*, Lean and Hinrichsen, Helicon, 1992, figures 8, 9, 12, 13 and 14.

Contents

Introduction

The IELTS examination

The International English Language Testing System examination (IELTS) is taken worldwide by students who intend to study in an English speaking country. There are about 35,000 candidates every year. IELTS is recognized by higher education institutions throughout the world as a measure of competence to study in the medium of English.

The tests

The IELTS examination assesses how well you can understand and use the kind of English you need to study in an English speaking country. There are four tests which all candidates have to take: listening, reading, writing and speaking. The tests are always taken in this order, and the first three tests are always taken in one day, with the speaking test taken on the same day or up to two days later. Each test focuses on a different skill:

- You will need to understand spoken English in both everyday life and much more formal situations, such as lectures and seminars. The **listening** component of IELTS assesses how well you can do this;

- When you study you will not have time to read all the books on the reading lists. So you must be able to find important information quickly and accurately from a number of sources. The **reading** component of IELTS assesses how well you can do this;

- When you have collected your information and your thoughts you will be asked to present your ideas as a formal essay or report. The **writing** component of IELTS assesses how well you can do this;

- You will also need to ask for information, to talk about yourself and to express your ideas in a variety of situations. The **speaking** component of IELTS assesses how well you can do this;

- While you are studying, researching or working you will constantly be under great time pressure to find information, think quickly and respond appropriately. Throughout, IELTS assesses how well you can do all of these.

The modules

The listening and speaking tests are the same for all candidates but the reading and writing sections of IELTS are available in two different modules: academic and general training. All candidates choose **one** of these modules depending on the kind of course they intend to follow.

(For more detailed information see the *IELTS Handbook*, which should be available at your local IELTS centre.)

IELTS is not designed to assess your specialized knowledge and you may not get questions from your own particular field. You should not worry about this. What IELTS tests is your English.

Scores

You do not pass or fail with IELTS. You are given a band score which shows your ability in each of the four tests and an overall band. When you apply to a university or college, they may specify which band you must achieve to be accepted on the course. Refer to the *IELTS Handbook*, available from your local IELTS centre, for a description of the overall band scores.

How to apply

For information on where and how to apply for the examination refer to the *IELTS Handbook*.

How to use this book

This book (and the tape that goes with it) provides advice and practice in the skills you need to do your best in IELTS. Like the examination, it is divided into four sections: reading, writing, listening and speaking. In each section you will:

- practise what you need to know;
- learn what to expect;
- get advice on exactly what you need to do in the test;
- become familiar with the type of questions you will get.

The main part of each section is called practice and consists of exercises which are designed to give you practice in **what you need to know** for each test: the major skills you need. By practising these you will at the same time be practising a number of useful subsidiary skills. Most of the exercises are based on the sort of questions you will get in IELTS. This is so you know **what to expect**. It is very important:

- to follow instructions carefully;
- to keep to the time limit;
- not to consult the answer key until you are told to do so.

Again, the instructions for questions are similar to those in IELTS. This is part of what you are practising. To build up as much practice as possible in the type of questions and instructions you will find in IELTS, and the processes you will go through in finding the answers, we have put the reading and writing sections before the listening.

Timing is also important, particularly since you will not always be told how much time to spend on individual questions in IELTS. Answers to the reading and listening exercises, as well as some of the writing exercises, and a transcript of the listening exercises, are in the back of the book. At the end of most exercises there is a discussion section, where you can look back on your answers and see how you can improve. Information about **what you need to do in the test** is covered in this section and is highlighted. This is also where you will find guidance on the **type of questions** you can expect.

This book is not an English course. You can and should continue to work on your grammar and vocabulary in whichever way suits you. At the end of each practice section there is advice on what sort of further work will help you in IELTS and there is a bibliography which lists useful books.

At the end of each section there is a summary of the main points in the section.

The book is aimed at candidates for the academic module. But it uses a variety of materials and reading passages which will allow you to practise the skills required in whichever module you are taking.

You can work through the book on your own, with other students or with the help of a teacher. The exercises in the speaking section are designed for two people working together. There is no space in the book for you to write answers so you will need to prepare your own answer sheets. You will need paper and you will need to number your answers.

Section one: practice

Reading

The IELTS reading test lasts for sixty minutes and assesses how well you can understand the type of texts you will find in the course of your studies.

The question booklet contains three reading passages (sometimes illustrated with graphs, tables or diagrams), and each passage has accompanying questions. The texts, which tend to increase in difficulty throughout the paper, vary in length, and so does the number of questions on each passage. The passages are usually from 500 to 1,000 words long for the academic module and somewhat shorter in the general training module. There is a total of about forty questions in all. Sometimes these come before the reading passage, sometimes after.

There is a wide range of different **question types**. You may be asked to:

- fill in gaps, for example in a passage of written text or in a table;

- match headings to written text or to diagrams or charts;

- complete sentences;

- give short answers to open questions;

- answer multiple-choice questions.

Sometimes you will need to give one word, sometimes a short phrase and sometimes simply a letter, a number or symbol.

It is important that you control the time on each reading passage. If you spend too long on one, you may not leave yourself time to complete the others. This is also true of individual questions. You will have to work very quickly; if you cannot do a question, leave it and go on to the next. When sixty minutes have finished, you will have to stop writing immediately.

Practice

In IELTS you are not reading for pleasure. You must identify what the question requires, find the information quickly and answer accurately. **You will not have time to read every word of every passage slowly and carefully**. You should not attempt to do this.

This means that you must develop ways to read quickly and efficiently. The first thing to do when you look at a reading passage is to survey the passage to find out what it is about in very general terms. If you understand the general subject it will help you later when you look for detailed information. You will know what to look for and where to look for it.

Exercise 1

Survey the following passage and answer the questions which follow:

Time: 2 minutes

Hidden history; the beetle's secret cycle of life

The deathwatch beetle is thought of as the devil's pest in churches and old houses, but in natural habitats it infests a wide range of decaying hardwoods. It has been found in hornbeam, sweet chestnut, hawthorn, beech, ash, blackpoplar, elm, larch, spruce and yew, but the two most commonly infested species in Britain are oak and willow. In buildings, oak timbers are usually the focus of attack by the beetle, but alder, walnut, elm, larch and Scots pine can be affected too. Deathwatch beetles attack wood that has been decayed by fungi, so it is the damp-prone parts of timbers, at the ends and near leaking gutters and enclosed spaces, that are normally attacked first.

Adult beetles emerge from holes in the timber in spring, or occasionally in autumn. They breed once and a week or two later the females lay eggs, usually about fifty, in small cracks on the surface of the wood. Adults depend on stored reserves; they do not feed, so the adult lifespan is largely determined by body size and metabolic demands. Emergent females rarely live for more than ten weeks, and males eight or nine weeks, at a temperature of about 20° C.

The eggs hatch after two to five weeks and the larvae then wander across the wood to find suitable entry points through which to bore into the timber. Then they take between two and ten years to complete their development. The larvae pupate in late summer to

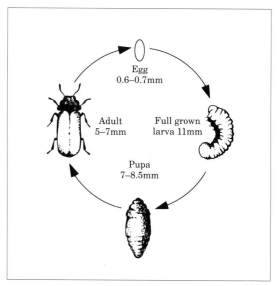

Figure 1

early autumn, each individual having constructed a pupal cell just below the surface of the wood. After two or three weeks, the immature beetle emerges from the pupal skin, but then remains torpid inside the chamber until the following spring or early summer. The mature beetle then cuts a perfectly round hole, three to five millimetres in diameter, and emerges covered in a fine layer of wood powder.

Questions 1–4

1   What is the subject of the passage as a whole?

2   Which paragraph contains information about the larvae?

3   Which paragraph contains information about the adult beetles?

4   Which paragraph contains information about where the beetles live?

Now look at the answer key and go on to the discussion section below.

Discussion

Notice how with only the title and the illustration you have most of the information in the passage. There may be many words you do not know in this passage but the title told you the topic was the life cycle of something. Figure 1 shows you what it is and gives you much of the key information.

Looking at the first sentence of each paragraph gives you enough information to answer questions 2–4 above.

You did not need to read every word and you did not need to *know* every word. This exercise practised surveying the text – which is something you should do with **every** text no matter what the questions are. This is a major reading skill. Some IELTS questions ask you to **find the main ideas** in a text. For this you go through the process of looking at the title etc., as you do when you survey the text. You have to recognize that this is what the question requires. In general you cannot answer a question properly unless you know what sort of answer is needed and how to find it. This takes us to the next main process you go through after surveying the text:

Analyse the questions

Ask yourself 'What is the purpose of this question?' If you can recognize that the question is asking about the general theme of the passage, then you already know how to find the answer quickly. If the question is asking for specific information, make sure you are clear what that information is (is it a number? a period of time? an activity? etc.).

Analysing the question has another meaning too. It means **read it carefully** to see what form your answer should be in (one word? two words? a sentence?).

Exercise 1 consists of the simplest kind of question type: **open questions**. You can answer in any number of words – there are no special instructions. You do not need to write full sentences. In fact, it is better to save time by just writing one or two words. Questions 2–4 can all have one-word answers, or simply a number.

Now you have surveyed the text you are better prepared to look for more detailed information. Go on to the next exercise.

Answer the following questions on the passage *Hidden history: the beetle's secret cycle of life.*

Time: 5 minutes

Questions 5–10

Complete the summary below by choosing a **maximum of two words** from the passage to fill the spaces 5–10. Write your answers on the answer sheet.

Summary

The deathwatch beetle is found most often in … **5** … and … **6** … They infest damp-prone timber which has been affected … **7** … Adults do not feed, so they survive on … **8** … and live for only two or three months. The larvae, on the other hand, live for up to … **9** …, feeding on the timbers during that time. They pupate in … **10** … but the adult does not emerge until the following spring.

Now look at the answer key and go on to the discussion section below.

Discussion

Most of the questions in the reading test ask you to **find specific information**. The best way to prepare yourself for this is by going through the first two processes properly:

- survey the text;

- analyse the question.

For example, because you have surveyed the text you should know exactly which paragraphs to look at for the answers to each question. This saves a lot of time. Also from analysing the questions you can often see what sort of information to look for. It is clear, for example, that the answer to question 9 must be a period of time.

So the first two processes are very important: you survey the text and you analyse the questions. Then:

> **Go back to the text to find the answers to the questions**
>
> Do not read every word and do not worry if you do not understand everything. Remember you are reading for a purpose. Be clear about what information you need to find and just look for that information. You will need to do this quickly.

Exercise 2 is an example of a typical **gap-filling exercise**. There are several important points to note:

- the passage in the exercise is a summary of the reading passage, so you will find many changes from the original;

- even if you find specialized words in the reading passage (e.g. 'pupate') you will be able to answer the questions (e.g. question 10); as stated in the introduction, IELTS is a test of your understanding and use of English, not your specialized knowledge;

- the question states that you must use a maximum of two words – you have to make a choice in question 10 between the two possible two-word answers given in the answer key – you cannot have both;

- the question states the words must come from the passage – you cannot use your own words.

The last two points show how important it is to **read the instructions carefully** and to check that you have done so. This brings us to the final process in doing the reading test:

Check your answers

Allow a short period of time for checking.

Look at any answers you are not sure of.

Read all the instructions again and make sure you have followed them exactly.

These are all the major skills you need to know and the things you need to do for the reading test. In the following exercises you will practise these skills and processes on other reading passages, and you will also meet some other types of question.

Exercise 3

Read the passage below and answer questions 11–15 which follow.

Time: 5 minutes

How the brain reorganizes itself

Paragraph 1

The work that Tim Pons and his colleagues published last week is basic research into the portion of the brain, the cortex, that one scientist says is 'responsible for all the interesting things we do'. The cortex is a layer between two and five millimetres thick that covers the brain and each area of the cortex has a different function. The area Pons and his colleagues are interested in receives 'somatic' sensation, in other words, information about touch, position, heat, cold and pain. The somatic sensory cortex can be represented as a topographic map, sub-divided into specific regions that receive nerve signals from specific areas of the body.

Paragraph 2

About twelve years before Pons and his colleagues carried out their experiments, the Macaque monkeys being studied had the nerves cut which carried signals from the fingers, palm, upper limb, neck and the back of the head. The regions bordering this part of the somatic sensory cortex receive signals from the face and trunk.[1]

Paragraph 3

Under anaesthetic, Pons and his colleagues inserted electrodes into the region of the cortex where the nerves had been cut and recorded the neuronal[2] response. They found to their surprise that the whole region, covering an area of between ten and fourteen square millimetres, now responded to stimulation of the lower face. Previously, scientists had thought that the cortex of adult animals could not reorganize itself over an area greater than one or two millimetres.

[1] trunk = the main part of the body
[2] neuronal = areas of the nerves

Questions 11–13

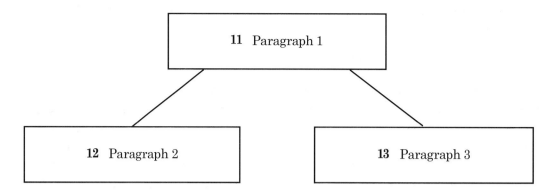

11 Paragraph 1

12 Paragraph 2

13 Paragraph 3

The diagram above represents the reading passage *How the brain reorganizes itself*. Match one of the headings below to the subject of each of the paragraphs in the reading passage. Write the corresponding letter in the appropriate space on your answer sheet. Note there are more headings than paragraphs so you will not use all of them.

List of headings

A   Macaque monkeys   B   Method of research

C   Electrical stimulation   D   The effects of heat

E   Cortex reorganization   F   The area of research

Questions 14–15

14   According to the passage, which four of the senses listed below are 'somatic' sensations?

A   taste   B   touch   C   temperature

D   pain   E   position   F   emotion

G   smell   H   sound   I   vision

Write the four appropriate letters (from A–I) on your answer sheet.

15   Which part of the brain receives signals from different parts of the body? Write up to three words from the reading passage on your answer sheet.

Now look at the answer key and go on to the discussion section below.

Discussion

Did you do the following?

● survey the text;

● analyse the questions to see exactly what they are asking for;

● read the instructions carefully;

● notice which questions were about general themes and which were asking for specific information;

● know where to look for specific information and what sort of information was required;

● go back to the text looking quickly for the information you need;

● remember not to try and read every word;

- move on to the next question if you could not answer one;

- leave enough time to check your answers and to check that you followed the instructions exactly.

Use this checklist for the next exercise you do.

You often find block diagrams (like questions 11–13) in IELTS. Questions 11–13 are typical of the **matching exercises** you find in IELTS. In this case you must identify the main theme of each paragraph or section. So these questions were about the **general themes** of the passage. It is not enough if a subject is mentioned; it has to be the dominant theme or idea. Paragraph 1 mentions heat, for example, but it is not about heat. Paragraph 2 talks about an experiment on Macaque monkeys but it is not about Macaque monkeys in general. The main point of paragraph 3 comes in the last rather than the first sentence.

Question 14 is a type of **multiple-choice** question: you have to choose the correct answers from a list. It is also a question where you must find **specific information** in the relevant paragraph. Notice that the actual text will not necessarily use exactly the same words as the question ('temperature' is not a word in that paragraph). It is the information you have to look for, not the words.

Question 15 seems very simple. But the important thing is to read the question very carefully: you must not use more than **three words**, and they must be **from the passage**.

Once again, do not worry about specialized vocabulary or knowledge: you may find a glossary of definitions of specialized vocabulary ('[1]trunk, [2]neuronal'); you can answer question 15 correctly without any previous knowledge of areas of the brain or their function.

Exercise 4

This reading passage contains some very long, complex sentences (more complex, in fact, than you are likely to find in the IELTS test). Don't panic. Use your checklist. Concentrate on identifying the key phrases and ideas.

Answer the questions below by reading the passage.

Time: 10 minutes

Social and cultural impacts of tourism in Cyprus

In Cyprus, hospitality forms an integral part of the culture, and the people have a welcoming attitude towards foreigners. Furthermore, the society's culture emphasizes ideologies and value systems which attach great importance to individual achievement. As the tourist policy followed by the Cyprus Government and the Cyprus Tourism Organization has been to aim at the middle and high income groups, and the tourists come mainly from Europe, tourism has not had as marked an adverse effect on the values and attitudes of Cypriot society as may otherwise have been the case. In certain areas, such as Ayia Napa, however, the influx of large numbers of tourists has influenced social behaviour and social values, and caused a certain amount of antagonism. Bryden suggests that:

> *there may be a relationship between tourism density, expressed in the annual numbers of tourists as a proportion of the population … and the growth of resentment towards tourists. … The inference here is that tourism density is an indicator of the degree of confrontation between tourists and indigenes and that this confrontation gives rise to the resentment of tourists.*

Table 1 Contact ratio values, 1985

Area	Contact ratio	
	Annual average	*Peak day value*
Limassol	19.5	7.3
Larnaca	24.4	13.9
Ayia Napa/Paralimni	3.0	1.5
Paphos	17.7	10.8
Hill resorts	43.0	16.6
Total	**18.0**	**9.5**

The concept of 'tourism density' is thus used as a measure of 'social carrying capacity' which Mathieson and Wall define as 'host peoples' levels of tolerance for the presence and behaviour of tourists'. An alternative measure used by Andronikou is the 'contact ratio', which is the inverse of tourism density, that is the ratio of the local population to tourist population. Now, whereas Andronikou suggests that the minimum value that the contact ratio can fall to before the social impact resulting from tourist development becomes detrimental is about eight, most authors now do not believe that a single specific value can be given for social carrying capacity. Mathieson and Wall point out that:

> *Carrying capacity remains an elusive concept, but the time when researchers and managers sought one mythical magic number, which could be approached with safety but exceeded at peril, has passed.*

Nevertheless, inspection of table 1 does suggest that it is highly likely that the social carrying capacity in Ayia Napa has been overreached. The extreme concentration of tourists here has resulted in a modification of social attitudes among young people, especially towards sexual behaviour. This is part of the 'demonstration effect' which introduces foreign ideologies and ways of life into societies that have not been exposed to tourist lifestyles. The close and continued contact of Cypriot youth with young foreign tourists has resulted in them adopting different sets of values on morality, style of dressing, and so on, in comparison with prevailing traditional attitudes, and as a result the bonds of closely knit families are in some cases being loosened.

Questions 16–18

Read the following statements and say how they reflect the information in the reading passage, by writing:

T   if it is true according to the passage,

F   if it is false according to the passage, and

NCG if the information is not clearly given in the passage.

Write your answers in boxes 16–18 on your answer sheet.

Example	*Answer*
Cypriots are welcoming	T

16   Individual achievement is more important than hospitality.

17   Tourists come mainly from the UK.

18   Cypriot society has not been adversely affected by tourism.

Questions 19–21

In the two lists below, a definition in the list on the right (A–G) matches one item in the list on the left (19–21). Show which items match by writing one appropriate letter (A–G) in boxes 19–21 on your answer sheet.

Example		*Answer*
'social carrying capacity'		C

19	'contact ratio'	A	ratio of locals to tourists
20	'tourism density'	B	introduction of foreign values to tourists
21	the 'demonstration effect'	C	host's tolerance towards tourists
		D	proportion of tourists to locals
		E	approximately eight
		F	introduction of new lifestyles into societies
		G	different sets of values

Discussion

Questions 16–18 are typical of the true/false type of questions that you may find in IELTS. Make sure you read carefully enough to answer the question accurately and make sure you answer according to the information in the passage. Both 'individual achievement' and 'hospitality' are mentioned in the opening paragraph; it does not state which is more important. You may know that most tourists in Cyprus come from the UK; the passage states 'Europe' only. For question 18, the passage states 'tourism has not had as marked an adverse effect …'. You may not know the meaning of 'as marked …'; the writer goes on to say, however, '… has influenced social … and caused … antagonism'.

Questions 19–21 are another type of matching exercise. In this case, you must match terms used in the text with possible definitions of those terms as used in the text. 'Tourism density' is '… expressed in the annual numbers of …' and '… used as a measure of …'; the former provides the definition.

Having found the definition of 'demonstration effect', you are wasting precious time if you try to understand the very long final sentence; you do not need to read it carefully.

Exercise 5

Sometimes the questions come before the reading passage. It makes **no difference** to the things you should do. Continue what you have been practising:

- survey the text;
- then analyse the questions;
- then return to the text.

In the next exercise some questions come before the passage and some come after it.

Answer the questions below by reading the passage *Hi-tech connections*.

Time: 7 minutes

Questions 22–23

Choose the most appropriate phrase from the two lists (A–D) and (E–H) to complete the two sentences below. Write the corresponding letters on your answer sheet.

22 Paragraph A is an introduction to …

A   management vocabulary   B   computers

C   high-technology communications   D   world markets

23 The purpose of paragraph C is to …

E   describe telephone networks   F   illustrate with an example

G   give a further example   H   introduce a new idea

Question 24

Complete the sentence below using a maximum of four words.

24 Rapid developments in advanced communications have resulted from …

Hi-tech connections

Paragraph A

Over the past fifteen years, information technology (IT) has become an essential part of the managerial vocabulary for a great many businesses. Today, however, telecommunications is rapidly becoming as important as the computer industry. This can be attributed to the liberalization of world markets, which has created an explosion in the development and availability of advanced communications services.

Paragraph B

In many instances, communications systems are being used to enable companies to implement new strategies. One such strategy is the move towards more globalized business. Obviously, setting up an office overseas is not simply a matter of identifying potential markets. Logistics, such as establishing links for the vital flows of information between a company's head office and its overseas subsidiaries and suppliers, are equally important. Not surprisingly, sophisticated communications systems play a fundamental role in connecting business operations.

Paragraph C

One such system is the Integrated Services Digital Network (ISDN), which enables companies to send and receive high speed data, fax transmissions and ordinary voice calls, as well as images for video-conferences, over international digital telephone networks. The network also enables businesses to offer their services on a worldwide scale. One such offering is the new International Dealerlink. This is a voice-only, private circuit service jointly offered by BT and France Telecom. It can meet the special communications needs of the finance community by providing a fast and cost-effective link between the two financial centres. The service also opened between the UK and The Netherlands at the end of January.

Questions 25–26

Using the information in the passage, answer the questions below using figures or a maximum of three words. Write your answers on your answer sheet.

25 What does 'such' refer to in the first sentence of paragraph C?

26 How many countries have access to the International Dealerlink?

Now look at the answer key and go on to the discussion section below.

Discussion

If you analysed the questions properly you will have seen that questions 22–24 focus on the **general themes** of the passage and paragraphs in it. Questions 22 and 23 deal with the topic and purpose of paragraphs. Question 24 took you further into the relationships within a paragraph. Questions 25 and 26 are both open questions requiring you to find **specific information**. Question 25 refers to relationships between paragraphs. It limits the number of words you may use but you may or may not choose to take them from the passage. For question 26 all you need to do is write down a number.

Questions 22–24 are examples of **sentence completion** questions: you have to complete sentences which are started for you. Pay special attention to the instructions. Questions 22 and 23 are both multiple-choice types of sentence completion: you are asked to choose the right phrase and put the corresponding **letter** on your answer sheet (you do not write out the phrase). Question 24 asks you to write the **phrase** which completes the sentence (you do not write the whole sentence); in fact the instructions state 'a maximum of four words' and writing the whole sentence would be marked as wrong.

Exercise 6

Sometimes graphs, charts, diagrams or tables will accompany the reading passage. Like figure 1 in the first exercise and table 1 in exercise 4, these can give you important helpful information about the text. The next reading passage provides another example.

Answer the questions by reading the passage below.

Time: 12 minutes

Perchance to dream

In 1952 the neurophysiologist Nathaniel Kleitman and one of his students, Eugene Aserinsky, studied the rolling movements of the eyes which occur early in sleep. They attached electrodes which responded to eye movements to the temples of volunteers who came to sleep in their laboratory. As the volunteers began to fall asleep, the electrodes detected the slow rolling eye movements which could be seen easily through their eyelids. Soon after, the volunteers fell deeper into sleep and their eyes became still. An hour or so later, to the great surprise of Aserinsky, the pen recorders showed that the eyes were moving again. This time they were not just swinging from side to side but were darting back and forth (see figure 2). These rapid eye movements continued for some time and then the eyes came to rest again.

These phases of rapid eye movement (R.E.M.) occur every ninety minutes or so and represent a distinct and important stage of sleep. The huge slow waves of normal sleep are replaced by a higher frequency pattern closer to the brainwaves of the normal waking state. In this state of 'paradoxical sleep', it is more difficult to wake the sleeper even though the brain is active. Indeed, most of the muscles of the body are paralysed, cut off from the restless activity of the brain by inhibitory signals from a tiny region deep in the brainstem. The only responses to the brain activity are the eye movements and the occasional twitching of fingers or the grinding of the teeth.

During this period of paradoxical sleep, vivid wild dreams usually occur. People deprived of this stage of sleep show many more signs of a sleepless night than if they have been woken at other times during sleep. Moreover, the following night they spend more time than usual in paradoxical sleep, as if they need to catch up on the dreams they had 'lost'. This discovery has led to the identification of regions within the reticular formation of the brainstem which might control this specific phase of sleep.

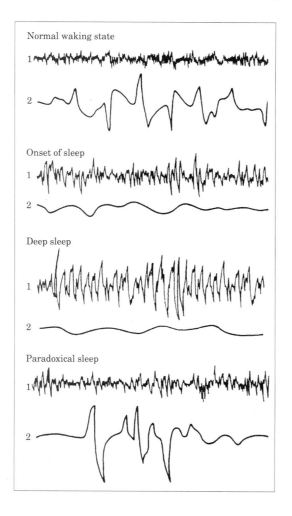

These signals were picked up with electrodes stuck to the scalp and face of a volunteer. In each case the upper trace (1) shows the electroencephalogram, which reflects the activity in the cerebral cortex, while the trace below (2) shows the movements of the eyes.

Figure 2

Questions 27–35

The block diagram below represents key information from the reading passage *Perchance to dream*. Complete the diagram by finding no more than two words from the text to fill each numbered space. Write your answers in the corresponding boxes on your sheet. If the information is not given in the passage, leave the box blank.

State	Brainwaves	Eyes	Body
waking	27		
onset of sleep	slower	28	29
30	31	32	33
paradoxical sleep	as waking	34	35

Questions 36–37

From the information in the passage, match the phrases A–D below with the brain pattern and physical evidence given. Write the appropriate letter in spaces 36 and 37 on your answer sheet. Note that there are more phrases than answers, so you will not need to use all of them.

A   rapid eye movement

C   vivid dreams occur

B   slow waves dominate

D   high frequency pattern

Brain pattern	Physical evidence
36	eyes roll slowly from side to side
very similar to the normal waking state	37

Now look at the answer key and go on to the discussion section below.

Discussion

Graphs and figures summarize information. Most of the information you need to check your understanding of the passage and answer the questions is contained in the diagrams.

You are often asked to provide answers by completing a flowchart or table, as you did for these questions. This is simply a different form of gap-filling exercise.

If you got any answers wrong and you do not know why, look again at the instructions. Questions 27–35 ask for not more than **two words** from the **text**. Question 37 asks you for **physical** evidence.

Once again, you did not need to give close attention to the final sentence; it contains no information relevant to the questions.

Exercise 7

Read this passage about a magazine called INFO and answer the questions which follow.

Time: 15 minutes

Desktop publishing

Desktop publishing (DTP) has fundamentally changed the way in which the business world looks at the production of documents, ranging from simple brochures and company reports to books, newspapers and magazines. Using a clever mix of computer technology, graphic skills and printing techniques it enables all kinds of organizations to provide high quality communication materials more quickly, simply and at a significantly lower cost than had previously been possible.

The first thing to note is that you do not have to be a publisher in order to benefit from DTP. It is used as much for improving the design and presentation of day-to-day documents as for producing publications. In order to understand the impact that DTP has made, it is necessary to understand the way in which INFO and other documents have been created using traditional methods.

The first stage in the old method of preparing INFO was the gathering together of all text, photographs and graphics which would make up the bulk of the magazine. The next step was marking the text for the printer – a rather laborious, and occasionally hit-and-miss affair! In essence, this meant judging the approximate length of the articles and choosing appropriate print sizes and styles (fonts). The appropriately marked pages were then sent to the printer for type-setting. The end-product of this type-setting phase is called a galley and takes the form of continuous columns on long sheets of paper.

At this stage the fun begins! All the columns of text have to be cut out and manually pasted onto sheets of paper marked out in columns, to give the layout for each page of the magazine. If one had misjudged the length of text at the type-setting phase, then screams of agony would mingle with the pervading smell of glue in the editorial offices as a very stressed editor wrangles bits of text and photographs. The flexibility of this old system was very limited, page layout was largely pre-determined and type-setting errors meant long and time-consuming proof-reading, both at the galley stage and at the final page proof stage. An additional problem with the old method is the length of time between the copy date (stage 1) and the publication of the magazine (about six weeks for INFO).

Desktop publishing made our life a lot easier. Now with our new system, we first type the text of the article on an ordinary wordprocessing package (MultiMate Advantage II is used but any other package is usable) or we ask our contributors to send us their article on a disk, typed with almost any word processor on an IBM or compatible PC computer. The second stage is to design the page frame, i.e. size, number of columns and margins. We then place the text in the page with an easy command called 'Autoflow'.

The third stage is the design of the layout: placing illustrations and choosing the most suitable typeface. At the last stage, we print the articles on the laser printer and pass them on to colleagues to be proof-read. After making all corrections, the files containing our next INFO are copied on to a disk and sent to our printers for publication.

As you probably noticed by the number of lines written to explain the two different methods, we are now able to save a considerable amount of time, effort – and glue!

Questions 38–44

Below are headings showing the stages involved in printing any document. According to the information in the passage:

write T if the stage is necessary in traditional printing;

write D if the stage is necessary with desktop publishing;

write TD if the stage is necessary in both methods.

Write your answers on your answer sheet.

Example: final printing   *Answer:*   TD

38   gathering input

39   designing page frame

40   marking text

41   type-setting

42   page design

43   cutting and pasting

44   proof-reading

Questions 45–47

Answer the following questions based on the reading passage.

Write your answers on your answer sheet.

Example: What kind of documents are produced with DTP?

Answer: brochures, reports, magazines.

45   How many factors are combined to create DTP?

46   What three advantages of DTP for organizations are mentioned?

47   What is sent to the printers with DTP?

Now look at the answer key and go on to the discussion section below.

Discussion

Questions 45–47 are open questions with no restrictions. You should have given short answers. The questions did not ask for sentences and you want to save as much time as you can. Question 45, for example, just needs a number. Sometimes more than one answer is possible, as in question 47.

Be very careful to answer questions by referring only to the information in the passage – not to any outside knowledge you may have. You may know that desktop publishing programmes have a command called 'cut and paste' but this information is not in the passage so it is not relevant to question 43.

If you do not have enough time or are not certain about the answer to a question, make sure you write **something**. There is no penalty for incorrect answers in IELTS and you do not get marks for blank spaces.

Exercise 8

This exercise is based on a full-length reading passage. It is broken into clearly marked sections, so your survey will be very straightforward. There is a wide variety of question types, so make sure you read the questions carefully and answer them accordingly. Prepare another answer sheet before you begin.

Read the passage and answer the questions which follow.

Time: 20 minutes

Reading skills

At university and college, all the four skills in English are important:

- *listening, for information in lectures, seminars and tutorials*
- *speaking, when taking part in seminars and tutorials*
- *reading, of textbooks, journals and handouts*
- *and writing, for essays and reports.*

Of these, reading is at least as important as any of the four. Students at tertiary level have a huge amount of reading to do; some for core information and even more as background to the main subject. It is therefore essential that it be done as efficiently as possible.

Written text has one distinct advantage over spoken discourse: it is static. Whilst this means a text can be reviewed as many times as the reader wishes, the rate at which any text is read will depend entirely on the speed of the reader's eye movements. Given the amount of reading that most students have to do, it is clearly in their interests to do so as quickly and as effectively as possible.

Obviously students must understand what they are reading. Less obviously, reading slowly does not necessarily increase comprehension. In fact, increasing reading speed may actually improve understanding. One thing to bear in mind is that reading, whilst being a receptive skill, is most certainly not a passive one. There must be an interactive process between the reader and the text in order to extract the meaning.

To illustrate this, some common misconceptions, and some common sense, are discussed below.

Vocabulary and discourse

Clearly one must have a command of the words of a language before comprehension can be achieved. There are, however, at least two other levels to be considered: syntax and discourse. It is almost pointless attempting to make sense of comprehensible lexis if one is not also very clear about how words are strung together in the target language. An understanding of word order, and the significance of changes in word order, are vital. The anticipation and recognition of common, acceptable and essential collocations clearly help the process of extracting information and meaning. Beyond this, it is also of paramount importance to recognize and understand the conventions of discourse structure, both generally and within specific subject areas. Recognizing the topic sentence in a paragraph, or the use of discourse sequence markers, for example, are the first important steps.

Eye movements

In practical terms, in order to read any passage, the eyes must follow the print on the page. This, however, cannot be a smooth, even flow; it would be impossible to focus on anything unless the eyes are momentarily fixed on the words. The eyes, then, must move in a series of pauses and jumps. There are several points to bear in mind with this process:

- the eyes and brain are so efficient that each fixation need last no more than a quarter of a second

- skipping back to re-read words is usually a result of anxiety and a feeling of insecurity; with confidence it can be eliminated almost entirely, instantly increasing reading speed.

It is very inefficient to read one word at a time. As mentioned above, collocation is very important; with practice, up to five words can be taken in at each fixation. Clearly this will increase reading speed dramatically.

Sense units

Reading slowly necessitates adding the meaning of one word to the meaning of the next, which is a very inefficient process. By reading in 'sense units', rather than one word at a time, concentration will be improved and meaning will be more easily extracted.

Using a guide

At school, children are often taught not to use their fingers as a guide while reading. If we wish to help our eyes follow the words efficiently, we can only gain by using some kind of visual aid. Whether we use our finger or another object, such as a pencil or a ruler, the only important thing is to increase the speed at which it moves across and down the page.

Skimming and scanning

With so much to cover, it is vital that students are selective in what they read. Skimming is a technique used in previewing or for getting an overview of a text; the eyes 'skim' rapidly over the page, just picking out the main ideas and topics. Scanning also involves rapid movement through a text, but looking for specific key information rather than the gist.

Practice

As with any skill, the more one practises the better one becomes. This will include both increasing the speed of movement of the visual guide and increasing the amount of text taken in at one fixation. Some move the guide vertically down the page, others diagonally; they all benefit. With practice it is not difficult, certainly when skimming and scanning, to take in two or more lines at a time. Moreover, as success comes with practice, confidence and motivation will increase also.

Fatigue

By reducing the backskipping and the number of fixations per page, the eyes will actually be doing far less work. This will reduce fatigue, thus allowing more to be read at one sitting.

Time

To sustain concentration and maintain efficiency, it is best to take regular short breaks. Most people find around half an hour of study is the optimum, followed by a few minutes to reflect before starting another period of reading. Regardless of the number of breaks, concentration is bound to fall to a counterproductive level after about two hours.

Question 48

In question 48 choose one of the answers below which best represents the information in the reading passage. Write the appropriate letter in box 48 on your answer sheet.

48   Which of the four skills is most important for students?

A   Listening
B   Writing
C   Reading
D   No single skill

Question 49

Answer question 49 by selecting *no more than three words* from the reading passage. Write your answer in box 49 on your answer sheet.

49   What is one advantage of written text over spoken discourse?   *It is static*

Questions 50–52

Read the following statements and indicate whether or not they reflect the information in the reading passage by writing:

T   if the statement is true according to the passage,

C   if it contradicts the passage, and

U   if it is unclear from the passage.

Write your answers in boxes 50–52 on your answer sheet.

50 The speed of a reader's eye movement is irrelevant.

51 Reading slowly increases comprehension.

52 Reading is a passive skill.

Questions 53–55

The paragraph below is a summary of part of the reading passage. Complete the summary by choosing a *maximum of two words* from the reading passage to fill the spaces numbered 53–55. Write the words in boxes 53–55 on your answer sheet.

The first one has been done for you as an example.

Summary: Reading skills

Example	*Answer*

Reading comprehension is a multi-level

skill: the reader must understand both

individual words and how they operate …   together.

Word order is very important in predicting and … **53** … the most usual combinations. To extract meaning quickly and effectively, it is also important to recognize conventional … **54** … and the importance of the … **55** … and discourse markers.

Questions 56–60

The paragraph below is a summary of the following section of the reading passage. Complete the summary by choosing the appropriate word, phrase or clause from the list below to fill the spaces numbered 56–60. Write the corresponding letter (A–N) in boxes 56–60 on your answer sheet. Note there are more choices than spaces, so you will not need to use all of them.

The first one has been done as an example.

Summary: Reading skills

Example	*Answer*

In reading, the eyes must follow

the printed text, but in order to …   F

clearly they must do this in a succession of very rapid … **56** … Confidence can reduce the amount of re-reading of words and with … **57** … the reader can fix on larger 'chunks', increasing reading speed and at the same time improving concentration and understanding. This process can be helped by using a visual guide whilst reading. To preview a passage, or to locate specific information … **58** … are useful techniques. Through practice, more can be read in a given time but for maximum … **59** … study periods should be broken into short sections of about … **60** …

List of words and expressions

A   a quarter of a second

B   regular short breaks

C   efficiency

D   backskipping

E   practice

F   focus

G   half an hour

H fixations

I improve comprehension

J pauses and jumps

K sense units

L skimming and scanning

M a guide

N two hours

Question 61

According to the information in the reading passage, which of the diagrams below best represents the eye movements of an efficient reader? Write the appropriate letter (A–D) in box 61 on your answer sheet.

A every day in every way

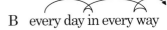

B every day in every way

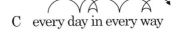

C every day in every way

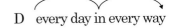

D every day in every way

Discussion

Questions 53–55 were a gap-fill of the type you have already practised; questions 56–60 were also of the gap-filling type, but this time you had to select from a bank of words and phrases. You may find both types in IELTS.

I hope you controlled your time and answered the questions accurately. Having used the passage for practice, you may now like to read it again more carefully and, where appropriate, use the information in it to improve your own reading skills.

Exercise 9

This is the last reading exercise. This time you have a full-length reading passage with questions before and after the passage. Be sure to use your time effectively and remember the checklist from the discussion section after exercise 3.

- Take two minutes to **survey** the text and **establish the general topic** and themes;

- **read the questions** and **instructions** very carefully;

- **find the specific information** quickly;

- **check** your answers.

The time you are given for this exercise is the maximum you should normally spend on any reading passage in IELTS.

  Time: 20 minutes

Questions 62–65

The list of headings below are taken from the reading passage, *Recruitment trends across the Channel,* which is in five sections. Choose the heading which is most suitable for each of the sections and write the corresponding letter in the spaces on your answer sheet. Note that there are more headings than sections so you will not need to use all of them.

List of headings

A   The future

B   Methods of recruitment

C   Problems of international recruiting

D   Head-hunting

E   The Euro-manager

F   The need for bilingualism

G   Developments in executive employment

H   Gross salary levels

I   Personality testing

J   The US in the single market

Example: Section 5   *Answer:* A

62 Section 1   **63** Section 2

64 Section 3   **65** Section 4

Recruitment trends across the Channel

Section 1

In the UK, there are three main types of professional recruitment organization: employment agencies, executive selection consultancies and executive search consultants. These three types of organization are geared to satisfying the needs of different levels of recruitment. Incidentally, all companies involved in the recruitment of personnel should be licensed annually by the Department of Employment. Additionally, it is totally illegal for any individual or organization to be remunerated by a potential recruit in return for finding a job.

Employment agencies cover the lower end of the salary spectrum and tend to concentrate on functional specializations – secretarial, accountancy, computer technicians, sales, etc., but will recruit up to junior management level. Generally, potential recruits register with the agency which then tries to place that person with one of its clients. Executive selection consultancies undertake a specific recruitment on behalf of a client, through advertisement. The consultancy will analyse the position that has to be filled, draw up an advertisement and advise the client of the most appropriate medium in which to advertise. Usually, the consultancy will handle the response and select a short list of the most suitable candidates. Such consultancies mainly operate by functional specializations and at junior to middle management levels.

Executive search, or 'head-hunting', can be described as the direct approach to a potential candidate with a view to recruiting that person on behalf of a client. Executive search is used for middle and senior management appointments.

Section 2

Psychometric tests are designed to evaluate numerous aspects of a candidate's personality and may include other assessments such as IQ, creativity and numerical skills. Such tests can be administered by the use of computers and may be as short as five minutes or may take a whole day. Graphology is the analysis of a person's handwriting to give indications of personality, state of health, intelligence and so on. Both forms of testing have received considerable attention over the last few years as companies have tried to make themselves more efficient in their methods of recruitment.

As with all forms of personality testing, neither sort of test is absolute. Many indications are open to interpretation and so can give false impressions or suggestions – the difficulty lies in deciding what is correct. Nevertheless, psychometric testing in the UK is seen as an important and useful tool in the recruitment procedure for senior executives. Most UK companies either have their own in-house testing facilities, or contract out to a single source of testing. On the other hand, graphology has never really caught on in the UK to the extent that it has in France. In fact, most UK managers would place greater faith in tea leaves!

Section 3

Despite the UK recession and the high levels of unemployment in both the UK and France, there has been an increasing willingness by employers to go outside their national boundaries in the search for suitable recruits. This is especially true in areas where specialist skill shortages exist, such as in certain disciplines of electronics and pharmacology.

With the advent of the single market, a number of companies, especially US-owned, are taking the opportunity of rationalizing their European operations. Rather than having a number of autonomous national subsidiaries, such companies are developing European headquarters or operations/co-ordination centres and are keeping what are, effectively, just regional offices in the various European countries. Such headquarters need to be staffed by managers able to work with several different cultures – the commonly called 'Euro-manager'. There is no doubt that there are increasing opportunities for such people to live and work abroad. Finally, the increased rate of redundancy amongst middle and senior management has produced, contrary to what might be expected, a perceptible change from advertised recruitment to the directed recruitment that constitutes executive search.

Section 4

Clearly, there are considerable difficulties involved in successful cross-Channel recruitment. Slowly, however, major French and British companies are becoming more aware of the benefits of having an international dimension to their senior management. It can be argued that major corporations, such as IBM and Rank Xerox, have long tried to give international experience to their senior managers. They usually rely on the company for facilities and support and on the expatriate community for social life. In contrast, the key factor in the personality of successful Euro-managers is a cultural sensitivity which permits them to recognize the strengths (and not only the weaknesses) of the various nationalities with which they work.

True fluency in two or more European languages is essential, together with the ability to communicate. Whatever their other abilities, however, the Euro-managers must, above all, be good at the job, whether it be in finance, logistics or sales. It is all too common to assume that linguistic ability can make up for mediocre[1] professional capability.

Section 5

Without a doubt, individuals must be prepared to be increasingly mobile and adaptable to different cultures, if they are to be really successful in the European employment market in the 1990s and beyond. Employers will be seeking all the qualities and skills already discussed as our national barriers break down. Such skills, are, however, in short supply today and identifying individuals possessing them is not easy. To recruit successfully across the Channel requires the existence of recruitment organizations whose staff have both extensive international experience and an excellent knowledge of their own national market. Clearly, they must have offices in the country where the client wishes to recruit, as well as having the ability to work coherently and to uniform standards.

There is no doubt that international recruitment is becoming more commonplace and so employers, potential employees and recruitment organizations must all ensure that they are prepared to meet the demands of the next decade and beyond.

[1] mediocre = not particularly good.

Questions 66–69

The table below contains key information from the reading passage *Recruitment trends across the Channel*, above. Complete the table by finding up to three words from the passage to fill each numbered box. Write your answers on your answer sheet.

Type of recruitment	Category of specialization	Level of management	Method of recruitment
employment agency	66	up to junior management	register
executive selection	functional	67	68
executive search	all types	middle to senior	69

Questions 70–71

Say whether the statements below reflect the information in the passage by marking your answer sheet as follows:

write T if the statement is accurate;

write F is the statement is not accurate;

write ? if the information is not given.

70 An increase in directed recruiting has been a result of the increase in redundancy amongst top executives.

71 IBM managers are provided with excellent social facilities.

Questions 72–73

Complete the following statements, based on the information in the reading passage above, using a maximum of three words.

Write the words on your answer sheet.

72 In electronics there is a shortage of specialists in …

73 Whereas psychometric testing is not absolute, it is …

Questions 74–75

Complete the statement below by choosing one of the phrases (A–D) from the list which follows.

Write your answer on your answer sheet.

74 In the second paragraph of section 2 of the reading passage above, 'neither' refers to

A   IQ creativity

B   short and long

C   personality and health

D   psychometric testing and graphology

75 What is the most important skill of a Euro-manager?

A language proficiency

B communication skills

C professional capability

D logistics

Answer by writing the appropriate letter on your answer sheet.

Question 76

76 According to the reading passage, how many factors are important for the success of organizations involved in cross-Channel recruitment? Answer by writing a number on your answer sheet.

Now look at the answer key and go on to the discussion section below.

Discussion

With a text of this length it is vital that you do not try to read every word. Instead you should go through the processes you have been practising. It is very important to **survey the text** properly. The way the passage was divided into five sections, and the way important terms such as *Euro-manager* were printed with capital letters, should have helped you in this. Did you go on to look at the topic of each paragraph?

If you **analysed the questions** properly you should have seen that questions 62–65 were about the general themes of the text. The other questions asked for specific information. Did you know where to look for it?

Did you **follow instructions** carefully? For example, you were given a limit on the number of words you could give in the answers to questions 66–69 and 72–73. Question 76 asked you for a number.

Finally, how was your **timing** and did you leave yourself time to **check your answers**?

This is the end of the practice section on reading. You have practised the different skills you need in the test and have had to respond to a range of different texts and question types. If you finished this last exercise in time and got the answers right, you are well prepared for the IELTS reading test. If not, you should go on practising your reading. Use 500 to 1,000 word texts dealing with interesting topics from a wide range of non-specialist publications appropriate to tertiary education. Practise the processes you have learnt (they are listed again in the summary section below). Always time yourself. Work with a teacher. Otherwise work with a partner or a group, if possible. Compare ideas and set each other questions on the texts.

The select bibliography gives a list of books which you may find helpful if you need to go on working on this part of the test. For further practice there are four test papers in section two, page 62.

Summary

What you need to **know**	What you need to **do**
How to understand main ideas	Survey the text
	Analyse the questions
How to find specific information	Go back to the text to find the answers to the questions
	Check your answers

Here are some points to remember:

1   Do not try and read every word: remember that you are reading for a purpose and do not worry if there is a word you do not understand – you may not need to understand it.

2   Look at the title and headings when you survey the text, as well as any special print such as CAPITAL LETTERS, underlining, *italics*, etc. and any figures, graphs, tables, etc.

3   Check that you have understood exactly what the question wants and that you have followed the instructions carefully.

4   Pay careful attention to your timing: do not spend too long on one passage or question – if you cannot answer a question, leave it and go to the next one.

5   If you are not certain about the answer to a question, be sure to write something – there are no penalties for incorrect answers.

Writing

The writing tests last sixty minutes and you have **two tasks** to do in that time.

In the **first task** you have to write a **description** of information usually given in a diagram. This may be an object, a set of data or a procedure. You have twenty minutes and have to write a minimum of 150 words. You need to present the description in a clear, logical and appropriate way.

For the **second task** you will be asked to write a clear **argument, discussion** or **report** on a given topic. You have to make use of your own knowledge and experience. You have forty minutes and have to write a minimum of 250 words. Again the argument has to be presented clearly and logically.

As in the other subtests, it is very important that you **analyse the tasks** carefully. You will not get marks for irrelevant material, no matter how much you write. It is equally important to control your **time**.

If you use information from one of the reading passages you must be careful **not to copy** sentences from the passage. You get no marks for copying.

You are given a booklet in which you have to write your answers. You may use a pencil to make notes but you may not use a dictionary. Your answers must be written in full sentences.

Practice

Most academic writing is in the form of reports and essays. In IELTS you will have two writing tasks: the first one is a simple description of an object, a process or some data, something you may have to write as part of a report; the other is an argument or a discussion on a given topic, which is more like an academic essay. In both tasks you will have to write in a clear, well-organized way and the same principles of good writing apply to both tasks. However, since the approach to task 1 and task 2 is slightly different this section will start with task 1 and move on to task 2 later.

Whatever you have to write about, you must make sure that your answer is relevant, that it actually does what you are being asked to do and does so appropriately. To do this you must read the task carefully to find out exactly what you have to do. Task 1 is simply a description of given information; it does not ask for any specialized knowledge or your opinion of the information. To produce a relevant answer you need to:

Analyse the task

This must be done quickly but carefully. You must read the instructions properly. The first academic writing task in IELTS is a description; you will therefore be asked to describe something. Analyse the task to find the **topic** or general theme. For example, in the following task: *Describe how solar radiation can be utilized to provide domestic hot water and lighting* the topic is solar radiation.

The next step is to decide on the actual **question** you are being asked. In the example above, the question is: *How can it provide domestic hot water and lighting?* The question is what you are being asked to write about.

You must also analyse the task to decide what particular **task type** it is, as this will affect how you organize your writing. This is discussed below.

Do not spend more than one minute on this.

Task 1 is a **description**. There are three types. You may be asked to describe a **process**, an **object** or a set of **data** (which may be a graph, a chart or a set of figures in a table.)

Process: With a process you must describe **how** something works or how it is made or used. The example on solar radiation asks you to describe a process (how it is used to provide hot water and lighting). For this you must focus on the **stages** in the process.

Object: With an object or set of objects you must describe **what** something is or what it does. For this you must focus on the **relationship** between parts.

Data: With data you must describe **changes, differences** or **trends**. Focus on **what** these are and **why**.

Exercise 1

Look at the task 1 titles below and then fill in the corresponding boxes to show the **topic** and the question for each of the tasks. Do not worry about the diagrams or tables that go with tasks: they are not necessary at this stage. The first one has been completed for you as an example.

1 Describe how solar radiation can be utilized to provide domestic hot water and lighting.

2 Describe the inner four planets of the solar system shown in figure 4.

3 Describe the life cycle of the beetle using the information in figure 1.

4 Write a brief report on unemployment in the United Kingdom 1988–1991 as shown in figure 5.

5 Describe the pattern and trends of tourist arrivals in Cyprus between 1977 and 1988.

Time: 5 minutes

Title	Topic	Question
1	Solar radiation	How can it provide domestic hot water and lighting?
2		
3		
4		
5		

Check your answers with the answer key before you read on.

Discussion

This takes us to the next process in selecting your material:

> **Write short notes**
>
> Once you have analysed the task and know what you need to do, the next step is to write notes. This is an essential part of organizing your writing and you should spend up to five minutes on this. **Choose relevant material** that you need to complete the description. What you choose must be relevant to the **question**.

Look at this task and diagram below and list all the **relevant** material you can think of in note form. (You do not need to write full sentences.)

> **Time: 5 minutes**

Describe how solar radiation can be utilized to provide domestic hot water and lighting.

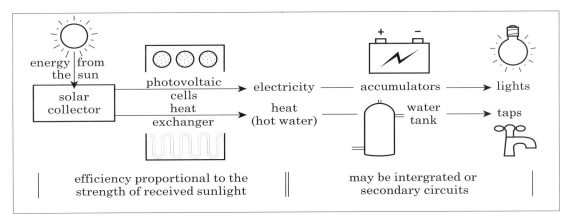

Figure 3

Discussion

It is impossible to give a complete list of correct answers to this exercise. Check your own answers, or check them with a friend or a teacher: are all the items in your list relevant to both the topic and the question?

Once you have a list of relevant items you need to **organize** them.

Arrange your notes under headings and order them

Rewrite your notes or mark them in some way to group them under **main headings**. This means putting your material into a **logical order**. How you do this will depend on the task type. For example, in the case of a **process** the logical order is to start at the beginning and follow the stages of the process through to the end. In the case of an **object** it is best to start with a general description and then focus on specific features. With a set of **data** you would generally describe the overall trend and then look at specific features. However you choose to do it, it is important to get your ideas organized. Otherwise you will not be able to write clearly.

Exercise 3

Using your notes from exercise 2 arrange them under **three or four headings** so as to order your material on the use of solar radiation to provide domestic hot water and lighting.

> **Time: 2 minutes.**

Discussion

There are at least two ways of organizing your notes for this question. One possible list of headings is given in the answer key. Check with a friend or a teacher that your headings are logical and clear. The question asks you to describe a **process** so your headings should follow the stages of the process.

Now try going through both the stages of **making notes** and **ordering** them for another task 1 question which asks you to describe a process. You should look at figure 1 in the reading section to do this. You may also refer to the reading passage which accompanies it, but remember **you must not copy from the passage**. You will get no marks in the writing test if you copy from a reading passage, so you must make sure you do not copy even when you are taking notes.

Exercise 4

Make notes and arrange them under headings for the following task: *Describe the life cycle of the beetle using the information in figure 1, page 10.*

Time: 5 minutes.

Discussion

Once again you should check with a friend or a teacher that your notes are relevant to the topic, the question and the task and that your headings are logical. You should have organized your notes to follow the stages in the process. You should not have copied sentences from the reading passage.

Now continue with the next three exercises, which ask you to describe objects and data.

Exercise 5

Make notes and arrange them under headings for the following task: *Describe the inner four planets of the solar system shown in figure 4.*

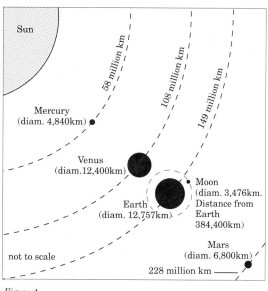

Figure 4

Time: 5 minutes

Exercise 6

Make notes and arrange them under headings for the following task: *Write a brief report on unemployment in the United Kingdom 1988–91 as shown in figure 5.*

Time: 5 minutes

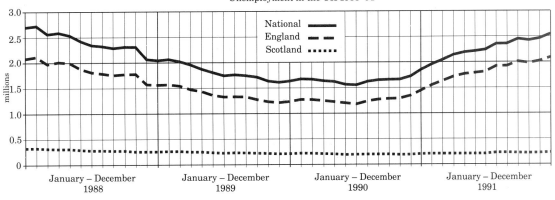

Unemployment in the UK 1988–91

Figure 5

Exercise 7

Make notes and arrange them under headings for the following task: *Describe the pattern and trends of tourist arrivals in Cyprus between 1977 and 1988.*

Time: 5 minutes

Table 2 Composition of tourist arrivals by age and sex (%)

Age/sex	1977	1983	1988
Age			
Under 15	14.3	11.7	9.5
15–29	25.9	24.7	26.1
30–44	33.1	30.5	27.1
45–59	18.9	22.1	24.4
60 and over	7.9	10.3	11.9
Not stated	0.0	0.7	1.0
Sex			
Male	58.8	53.6	49.0
Female	41.2	46.4	51.0

Discussion

Once again, you will have to check your answers with a friend or teacher. Make sure that you choose relevant material and that you organized your notes properly. For exercise 5 you should have ordered your notes to describe the system as a **whole** and then the different planets **individually** in sequence. For exercise 6 you should not have made notes about every point in the graph. Instead you should have described **general trends** and focused on **particular points** where significant changes took place. In exercise 7, you will have noticed that there are opposing trends in both categories, age and sex. Again, describe the trends and particular figures which do not fit, rather than every figure in the table. Whenever you describe a set of data you will have to be particularly careful about what material you select and what order you present it in.

Ordering your notes, which you have been practising, is part of the second important writing skill: **organizing your ideas**. As you have seen, this starts when you make notes. It extends into the actual writing process. Good writing is clearly organized. There are many ways in which you show the reader how you have organized your ideas.

- divide your answer into **paragraphs**, with one paragraph for each of the main headings in your notes;

- within each paragraph, write clear **sentences**, with one sentence for each item in your notes;

- use **linking words and expressions** to show how you are organizing your ideas: show the order of events with time expressions (first, next, etc.) and the relationship between parts with comparatives and superlatives (the larger section, the most important bit, etc.) and with prepositional phrases (next to, linking these ... , etc.). See relevant sections of books in the bibliography for information and practice;

- for task 2 it is important to **begin** and **end** clearly as well as giving clear **examples**. This is discussed further below;

- **punctuation** is another way of organizing your writing clearly.

After you have analysed the task, selected material to make notes and ordered your notes, you are ready for the next stage:

Write

Use your notes and pay particular attention to what has been said about **organizing your ideas** clearly.

Exercise 8

Choose one of the task 1 titles 1–5 in exercise 1 for which you have made notes and write a full answer from your notes. Check that your notes are in a logical order and make sure you organize your writing to show the order. Pay particular attention to paragraphs, sentences, linking expressions and punctuation.

Take a maximum of 10 minutes and make sure you write a minimum of 150 words.

If you take 5–6 minutes making sure you understand the question, making your notes and ordering them, and 10 minutes for the writing, then you will have some time to check your own written work before going on to the next task. When you have finished, check your answer with a friend or a teacher. Now repeat exercise 8 for the other tasks for which you have made notes. Time yourself and again check your answers with a friend or a teacher.

Task 2 is the second and longer task in the writing test. It differs from task 1 in that you are asked to present an **argument** for or against a point of view. So there is more scope to express your own ideas and opinions. However, you should be careful to present your views clearly and in the form of a logical discussion. Do not be emotional. Everything that has been said about the importance of analysing the task, selecting material and organizing your writing applies equally to task 2 and there are some extra points which will be discussed.

For task 2 it is very important to go through the first process (analyse the task) very carefully. Very often the question is not easy to see. Look at the titles 6–8 below. You will see that in each case the title consists of two statements. Often one of the statements is factual and the other is subjective (a matter of opinion). It is the **subjective** statement that is the actual **question**. In title 6, for example, there is a factual statement (*Modern high-technology is transforming the way we work*) and a subjective statement (*is of benefit to all of society*). You could give examples of high-technology and new ways of working (the **topic**) but what you are really being asked to discuss is *whether or not it is of benefit to all of society*. You will see that it can be expressed in the form of a **question** (*is it of benefit to all of society?*) and it is this question that you are being asked to discuss.

Look at the titles below and decide whether they contain factual or subjective statements and what the topic and question is. Fill in the table. The first one has been done for you.

Time: 2 minutes.

6   Write an essay for a university lecturer, arguing either for or against the following statement: *Modern high-technology is transforming the way we work and is of benefit to all of society.*

7   Write an essay for a university lecturer on the following topic: *Higher mammals such as monkeys have rights and should not be used in laboratory experiments.*

8   Write an essay for an educated non-specialist on the following topic: *More and more young people are studying and working overseas and this will help to bring about greater international co-operation in the future.*

	Title	Topic	Question
6	Modern Tech + Work	The changes modern high-technology is making to the way we work	Is it of benefit to all of society?
7	Experiments on Animals	Higher mammals have being rights used in lab.	Should they be used in lab exp?
8	Working + Studying Abroad	More + more young people studying + working overseas	Will it bring about greater international co-op.?

When you have filled in the table look at the answer key and go on.

It is particularly important in writing task 2 to display clear thinking and organization. You should go through the processes you have been practising, taking notes and organizing your writing – but in addition you should remember to:

- make it clear **which side** of an argument you are presenting (use clear linking expressions such as 'On the one hand … On the other hand') and make sure you do not mix two sides of an argument in the same paragraph;

- make it clear when you are giving your own **opinion** (use expressions such as 'in my view … ');

- have a clear **introduction** telling the reader briefly what areas you are going to cover and a **conclusion** which sums up the argument (make sure you organize your notes so that you have an introduction first and a conclusion last);

- give examples clearly (choose good examples which illustrate your argument when you take notes, and when you write introduce them with phrases such as 'For example … ').

Make clear ordered notes, including your own examples at relevant points, and a clear introduction and conclusion on one of the tasks 6–8 above.

Time: 8 minutes

Now write an answer from the notes you made in exercise 10. Pay particular attention to organizing your ideas clearly and the different ways of doing this which have been discussed.

Take a maximum of 20 minutes and make sure you write a minimum of 250 words.

When you have finished exercises 10 and 11 check your answers with a friend or with your teacher. Now repeat exercises 10 and 11 for the other two tasks from 6–8 above. Time yourself and check your answers with a friend or a teacher.

As well as writing a clear, relevant answer it is important that your English is **accurate**. You should ensure that you write in an appropriate **style**, and that your **grammar** and **spelling** are correct.

Style:	In task 1 you have to give a fairly technical description. In task 2 you must write an essay or argument for a university teacher, a report to a superior, or an essay for a non-specialist reader. For both tasks you must use **formal academic English**. Write formally even when stating your own ideas; make use of the passive for descriptions and use full forms (e.g. *they are* rather than *they're*);
Grammar and spelling:	You must remember to use appropriate tenses and ensure that your subjects and verbs agree. Check the use of prepositions and articles, that you have the correct form for adjectives and adverbs, and, of course, your spelling. If you have particular problems with any of these consult a grammar book (see the bibliography). If you do not notice your errors while you are writing, you will have a chance to correct them during the final process.

Check your answers

As for the reading, you should make sure you allow yourself a short time at the end of each question (about five minutes for task 1 and at least five minutes for task 2) to check your answers. You should use the time particularly to check that you have used **correct forms,** as well as to make sure that you have written the required **number of words** (150 words for task 1 and 250 words for task 2).

Read the following extract from an answer to exercise 9 task 6, which was written by a student and contains many errors:

Modern technology is transforming the way we work and is of benefit to all of society.

The modern technology can transform all of society for example when you work in your farmer by machine you ern lots of produse. but you work withot technology you'll have a little so we have know the modern technology has benefit for us. but some countries haven't modern technology then they can not grow equal with some countries that use to modern technology like 3th word's countries.

- Correct the spelling.

- Check the grammar. In some cases you can simply correct the errors but you may have to rewrite some sentences entirely.

- Decide whether you need to add punctuation or appropriate link words, or to re-order sentences entirely.

- Check the style. Remember you should use full forms (*they are* not *they're*) in this type of writing.

   Time: 10 minutes

   When you have finished, check with the answer key for one possible version.

Discussion

This exercise shows you how important it is to check your work carefully, especially to make sure that you have used correct forms. For practice you should repeat exercise 12 with all the texts you have written so far. Time yourself and see how many errors you can find and correct within five minutes. Check your work with a friend or a teacher.

Exercise 13

To give you more practice on checking, here is an answer from a student to exercise 9 task 7. Look at the text and decide how well the student has performed:

1   Has the student analysed the question properly and selected appropriate material?

2   Have the ideas been organized clearly and logically? Is there a clear introduction and conclusion? Are examples given? Are there clear links between ideas?

3   What about style, grammar and spelling?

   Time: 10 minutes

Higher mammals, especially monkeys, have rights and should not be used in laboratory experiments

   People, or we can use 'human kind' use broadly in lab. experiments with animals, which means we get more sence of security while taking drugs, or making up when you've known they were tested by animals. No body would be pleased to try a new drug product that haven't been proved in a lab to cure their disease, because it is to say you are the 'testing sample', This's a social survice though, but seldom wants to do.

   Higher mammals, such as monkeys, are the nearest kind of human. The got feeling, emotion, and able to act what they want or not. How can people just kill them and pick their body organs out; or inject some material into their vassuls; even electrolyse those inosent, pure, helpless mammals which is just like killing a baby. If they spoke, they would shout: we are not going to be test in a lab!

   Unfortunately, present science technic is not able to change such situation still, But some are trying in modify computer program, if it works than we will have more opportunity to keep more mutual benefit of human and higher mammals. Stop murdering for they got the most similar body structure with people.

   When you have finished, check with the answer key.

Now you have practised all the major writing skills you will need and have looked at a range of different tasks. The final exercise is a complete writing exercise.

Complete the tasks below. Remember to control your time as well as the number of words you write. Go through all the processes in the time available.

For task 1, take a maximum of 20 minutes and make sure you write a minimum of 150 words.

For task 2, take a maximum of 40 minutes and make sure you write a minimum of 250 words.

Task 1

Using the information in table 3 about first year (group 1) and second year (group 2) engineering undergraduates at an Italian university, write a short report on the findings of the survey.

Table 3 Secondary education of engineering students at an Italian university				
Total number of students	**Group 1 (312)**		**Group 2 (254)**	
Secondary school attended	**%**	**Number**	**%**	**Number**
i) Institute for engineers	4	12	6	15
ii) Institute for accountants	3	8	0	0
iii) Technical institute	22	68	28	70
iv) Classical school	26	80	18	45
v) School for sciences	45	141	48	122
vi) Other	1	3	1	2

Task 2

Write an essay for a university lecturer on the following topic:

As most postgraduate research today is funded by industry then student grants should also come from the same source. Remember to include examples to illustrate your ideas.

Discussion

This is the end of the practice section on writing. If you wrote two good answers in the set time you are well prepared for the IELTS writing test. If you want more practice, set yourself tasks similar to those above, in your field of study or any area of general interest. Practise the main processes and always keep to the time limit. Work in a group if possible, exchange and compare ideas and set each other tasks. Ask a teacher to assess what you write.

The select bibliography may be helpful if you need more practice in this part of IELTS. For further practice there are four test papers and five supplementary writing tests in section two, page 62.

Summary

What you need to **know**	What you need to **do**
	Analyse the task
How to select material	Write short notes
How to organize your ideas clearly and logically	Arrange your notes under headings and order them
	Write
How to use correct forms	Check your answers

Here are some points to remember:

1   We can summarize the main processes as follows: **plan it, write it** and **check it**. Of these, perhaps the most important is the planning process, so make sure you analyse the task properly and spend some time making notes.

2   Remember if you include information from the reading passage(s) in your answer to task 2 you may use ideas from the reading passages but you should not copy word for word. **Copying word for word scores zero in IELTS**.

3   Finally, if you have not finished task 1 after 20 minutes, leave it and go to task 2. It is very important that you should always leave yourself enough time to do task 2 properly. It is longer than task 1 and **carries more marks**.

Listening

In IELTS the listening comprehension is designed to assess your ability to understand spoken English and is the same for all candidates. There is a pre-recorded tape which lasts for about thirty minutes. There is a total of about forty questions. There are four sections in the test. Each section contains four or five short, linked passages of about one minute each or one longer passage of up to four or five minutes. The passages get more difficult as you progress through the tape.

The earlier sections use situations in which you may find yourself on first arriving in an English speaking country, when you need 'survival English'. These include finding your way around, following directions, giving and taking down information, making arrangements, etc.

In the later sections, the topics usually concern education and training. Here you may have to do the kind of thing you will need to do in an academic environment – listen to pre-recorded information, listen to lectures, pick out relevant key information from a dialogue, and so on.

You will hear monologues, dialogues and conversations. You will hear male voices and female voices. You will also hear a variety of accents. You will hear the passages **once only**, as in most situations in real life.

You are given a booklet. This contains all the instructions and questions with space to write your answers.

As in the reading test, there is a wide range of question types, which you have practised in the reading section. Much of this may be in the form of graphics, such as tables. This applies also to multiple-choice questions, where you may have to choose between a number of pictures or mark a point on a plan. Spelling is important only where it is clear from the tape that accuracy is required, such as filling in important details on an application form. Generally, spelling and grammar are not too important as long as the examiner has no trouble deciding what you mean. Answers require notes, letters or numbers rather than complete sentences.

You will be given time to check your answers between sections, and at the end of the test, as well as some time to read the questions before each section. **Instructions are recorded on the tape**. They are clear and you are often given examples of what you have to do. At the end of the test you are given ten minutes to transfer your answers to an answer sheet.

Practice

Just as in the reading test you were reading for a purpose, so in the listening test you are **listening for a purpose**. Your purpose is to identify what the question requires, find the information efficiently and answer accurately. It is not necessary to understand every word that is spoken. Do not worry if there are a few words you do not understand.

You will hear the information once only. This makes it particularly important that you **prepare yourself** properly before you listen. When you listen you will have to work quickly. You must read the question, understand it, follow the recording, recognize the answer and write it down – while continuing to do all of the above for the next question. It is therefore important to **anticipate** what you will hear. You are given a short time to read the questions before each section. You must use this time.

Exercise 1

Look at questions 1–4 pages 47–49 for 30 seconds. Can you anticipate any of the likely **situations** and possible **topics**? Repeat the exercise for questions 5–10: a 30-second survey.

> **Compare your suggestions with the answer key. Then read the discussion section below.**

Discussion

This is like any listening situation, whether in a foreign language or in our mother tongue. When we have established the topic, we listen for key information only. If we know the topic, it will be much easier to identify what the key information is. This is the next skill.

You must know what **specific information** you are listening for: is it, for example, a time or a place, a fact or an attitude? Similarly, you must know someone is going to make points before you can listen out for them. In the recording you are only told when each section begins and ends. You are not told when to go on to the next question. You must decide that for yourself. This is another reason why you must be clear about what each question requires. To find the specific information you need, go through the following process:

Exercise 2

Look at questions 1–4 again for 30 seconds. What is each question asking you and what will you have to listen for? Repeat the exercise for questions 5–10.

> **Compare your suggestions with the answer key. Then read the discussion section below.**

Discussion

After this stage you should know what the recording as a whole is likely to be about and what kind of information you are listening for. This is *before* you do any listening. You will notice that the **question types** are similar to those in the reading test, so look back at the reading section if you need to remind yourself of what they are. Questions 1–4, for example, are just multiple-choice questions. The only difference is that instead of choosing a word or a phrase you are asked to choose a picture. You can expect a few picture multiple-choice questions at the beginning of the listening test. Now you are ready for the next important process:

Listen

Listen to the recording. Do not worry about understanding every word. Just listen for the specific information you are looking for. Write your answers down **as you hear them** but do it quickly and **keep listening** for the answer to the next question while you are writing. This is difficult but it is easier if you have analysed the questions properly so you know what you are listening for. If it is a dialogue make sure that you know who the characters are and who is talking at any particular time. This is easier if you have surveyed the questions fully.

As usual, the final process is:

Check your answers

You are given a short time at the end of each section and at the end of the whole test to check your answers. The tape will tell you when to do this. You should make use of this time to look over your answers and especially to check that you have followed instructions properly.

Now you are ready to listen to the tape and do the listening exercises.

Instructions are given on the tape. You may stop after each section and read the answers and discussion in the answer key. If you prefer to listen to it as a whole, let the cassette play on and look at the answer key at the end. There is a transcript of the recordings in the back of the book. You must not look at this until you have done the listening exercises.

There will be time for you to look at the questions before each section, to check your answers between sections and again to check all your answers at the end. The tape includes timed pauses to allow you to do this. Remember to go through the processes of surveying the questions and analysing them during the time you are given to do this. Check your answers carefully at the end. Start the tape when you are ready to begin.

Listening exercises

Section 1

Questions 1–4

Decide which of the pictures best matches what you hear on the tape and circle the letter for that picture.

The first one has been done for you as an example.

Example: What time is it now?

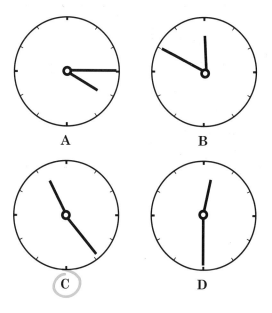

A

B

C

D

1   Which street plan shows the way from the station?

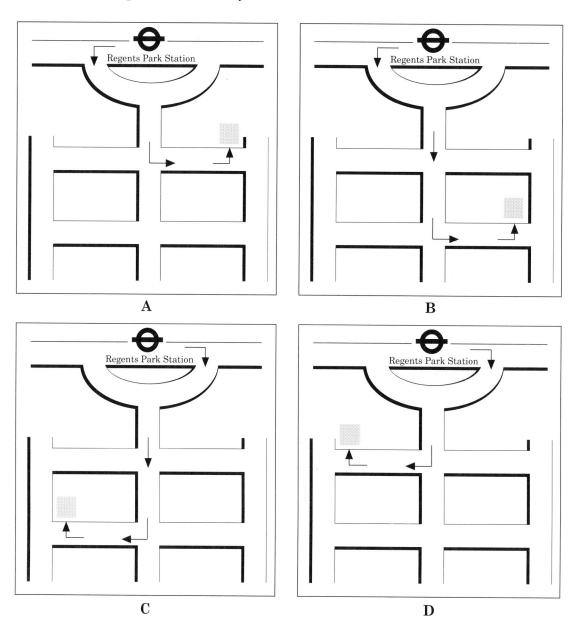

A

B

C

D

2   Which train is Abdul catching?

A	B	C	D
1144 London Victoria only	1134 London Waterloo only	1134 London Waterloo calling at: Ascot Richmond Vauxhall	1144 London Waterloo only

3   Which sign should Abdul follow?

Northern Line Southbound	Bakerloo Line Northbound
A	**B**

Northern Line Northbound	Bakerloo Line Southbound
C	**D**

4   Who is Abdul meeting?

A   B   C   D

Questions 5–10

Fill in the gaps numbered 5–10.

Central College Badminton Club

Family name: **5** ....   First names: .... *Abdul* ....

Faculty: ...... *Eng./Science* ....   Course: **6** ....

Year: (F) I   II   III   P   S.U.No. **7** ....

Term address: **8** ....

Standard: Mark one box only with an 'X'

9 .... ☐ beginner   ☐ average   ☐ good   ☐ league

Experience: Circle the appropriate number of years

10 1   2   3–5   5–10

That is the end of section 1. You can go on to the questions for section 2 or stop the tape here and check your answers in the answer key. If you pause and check your answers here, make sure the tape is in the right place (stop it immediately at the end of section 1) before you continue with section 2.

Now you can try a longer practice with a greater variety of question types. It is in three sub-sections, so you can do it in three parts if you find it difficult.

Start the recording before you read the questions. Use the time which you are given on the tape to survey and analyse the questions so that you can listen ahead. Begin when you are ready.

Section 2

Questions 11–12

Answer the questions by writing a word or number.

11 How many sections are there in the library? ....

12 Can all non-reference books be taken out for three weeks? ....

Questions 13–14

Put a tick (✓) in the appropriate boxes.

	Subject	**Author**	**Title**
13 Biblitas			
14 Micro-fiche			

Questions 15–17

15 Mark the diagram with an 'X' to show the position of the self-access centre.

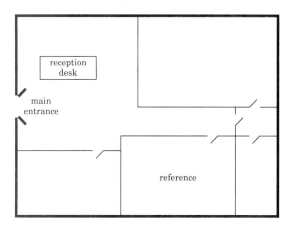

16 What equipment is fitted with headphones?

A   audio players   B   video players

C   audiolabs   D   satellite TV receivers

E   computer monitors

Circle the appropriate letter(s).

17 How many people can listen to the news on satellite television at any time?

A   2   B   5

C   6   D   12

  Circle the appropriate letter.

Questions 18–19

Write a word or number in the space provided.

18 Is it possible to use the library on Saturday evening? ....

19 In total, CALL disks are available in how many languages? ....

Question 20

20 Circle the appropriate dates.

Training sessions will be available on:

Monday	Tuesday	Wednesday	Thursday	Friday
		1	2	3
6	7	8	9	10
13	14	15	16	17
20	21	22	23	24
27	28	29	30	

  That is the end of section 2. You can go on to the questions for section 3 or stop the tape here and check your answers in the answer key. If you pause and check your answers here, make sure the tape is in the right place (stop it immediately at the end of section 2) before you continue with section 3.

Section 3

Questions 21–22

Complete the statements below. Use up to three words.

21 In the foundation year, students can take up to ....

22 The tutor asks Ana Maria why she has chosen ....

Questions 23–25

23 What does Ana Maria hope to do? ....

  Write a short phrase in the space provided.

24 When Ana Maria says she would not benefit from a foundation course in computer programming, the tutor:

A   disagrees and asks her to explain   B   agrees and asks her to continue

C   disagrees but asks her to continue   D   agrees and continues

  Circle the appropriate letter.

25 Ana Maria's reasons for taking art and design are:

A   accepted after discussion   B   rejected at first but then accepted

C   accepted at once   D   rejected

  Circle the appropriate letter.

Questions 26–28

Indicate whether the following statements are accurate or not by writing:

A for an accurate statement;

I for an inaccurate statement;

N if the information is not given.

26 Ana Maria has problems with reading and writing ....

27 The tutor suggests joining two different classes ....

28 The tutor suggests delaying German for one year ....

Questions 29–30

Give two ways it is possible to contact the tutor.

29 ....

30 ....

That is the end of section 3. You can go on to the questions for section 4 or stop the tape here and check your answers in the answer key. If you pause and check your answers here, make sure the tape is in the right place (stop it immediately at the end of section 3) before you continue with section 4.

Section 4

Questions 31–35

Fill in the gaps numbered 31–35 in the notes below

Notes: Study skills

Tertiary education: students are treated **31** ....

They have to be more independent and be responsible for their own decisions. They need, for example, to work out their own **32** ....
.... and keep to it.

Different classes: many students will not have taken part in seminars and **33** ....
.... at school.

Speaking skills: this does not mean pronunciation. It deals with the way people **34** .... This is needed when taking part in **35** ....
.... and will also be useful in writing.

Questions 36–38

Indicate whether the following statements are true or not by writing:

T   for a statement which is true;

F   for a statement which is false;

?   if there is insufficient information.

36 The lecturer gives an example of link words ....

37 The next lecture will be on ways of disagreeing ....

38 The lecturer divides the board into three columns ....

That is the end of section 4 and of the listening exercises.

In the IELTS test you would now have 10 minutes to transfer your answers to the answer sheet – make sure you write your answers in the appropriate spaces.

Check your answers and read the discussion sections in the answer key.

Discussion

This is the end of the practice session on listening. You have practised the different skills you need and have had to deal with a range of different questions. If you finished the listening exercises on time and got the answers right you are well prepared for the IELTS listening test. If not, you should go on practising your listening. You may be able to borrow recordings of lectures in English. If not, use study skills and other listening materials which are commercially produced and may be available in your library. (See the bibliography for suggested titles.) Listen to the radio, the BBC World Service, for example. Listen to plays and discussions as well as the news and information items. You will hear monologues in IELTS but you will also hear dialogues and conversations, in both formal and informal situations. Listen intensively in short bursts and attempt to make notes of what you hear. If you can record a programme it will make it much easier to check. If you are worried about numbers ('seventeen' or 'seventy'?), letters of the alphabet ('J' or 'G'?) or pronunciation and listening in general, refer to published material. There is no substitute for practice. Listen to whatever sources of spoken English are available to you, as often as possible.

In the IELTS test you would go on to do the reading and writing tests at this point. If you wish to simulate the test as closely as possible, you may now like to go on to one of the test papers in section two.

What you need to **know**	What you need to **do**
How to anticipate general content	Survey the questions
What to listen for	Analyse the questions
	Listen
	Check your answers

Summary

Here are some points to remember:

1   Do not try and listen to every word. Instead listen for the specific information you want: remember you are listening for a purpose. Do not worry if there is a word you do not understand – you may not need to understand it.

2   Check that you have followed instructions carefully.

3   If you do not know the answer to a question, move on quickly to the next question.

4   Even if you are not certain about the answer to a question, write something. There are no penalties for incorrect answers.

Speaking

The speaking test is an interview which assesses how well you can communicate in spoken English. It is a test of general speaking skills and is broadly the same for all candidates but you may also be asked to talk about your area of study. The interview lasts for twelve to fifteen minutes and is in three main sections:

- The first section is on general topics, such as your experiences and the differences between your home culture and the English speaking environment in which you will be working or studying.

- This is followed by a section where you are asked to find out information from the examiner by asking questions. You are given situations of the type you may find in your new work or study environment: asking directions, making appointments, finding out about meetings and so on.

- The final section focuses on your experience, study and future plans. You are assessed on your ability to communicate **fluently** and **accurately** using appropriate grammar and vocabulary. Your fluency is being assessed so it is important to **say as much as you can** as well as to speak spontaneously and **not to learn what you are going to say**. If the examiner thinks you are giving a prepared answer he or she will quickly change the topic. The interview may be recorded. This is to make sure the interviewers and band scores are consistent in all IELTS centres. In this part of IELTS there are no processes you have to think about: the examiner will take you through the test. Similarly you do not have to worry about timing, as the examiner will control the time.

For this section of the book it is essential to have a study partner – a teacher or another person to practise with. The exercises are designed for two people working together. There are no 'answers'; you and your study partner must assess how well you do. The tape contains some sample interviews by students. They are not 'model interviews' and you should not try to imitate them. They are included so that you can have a clearer idea of what to expect in the interview.

Practice

To get maximum benefit all the practice should be done **without preparing your answers**. You will not know exactly what the examiner is going to ask or exactly how he or she will ask it. You need to be **spontaneous**, to speak as **naturally** and **fluently** as possible. The aim of this practice section is to help you to prepare for the type of questions you will get and to practise dealing with them **without preparing specific answers**. It is important to keep to this for two reasons. First, the examiner will notice if you are repeating something you have learned and will stop you. Second, though it may seem difficult at first, it will actually make the test easier for you if you relax and talk naturally rather than trying to remember a ready-made answer. So the first and most important skill is **talking fluently**.

The only way to improve your fluency is by getting a lot of practice in speaking. Be confident. Think about **what you want to say**. Of course you should try to get your English right, but do not worry too much about getting everything absolutely correct. The important thing is that you should speak and listen, that you should engage in a real conversation with the examiner (who may be interested in what you have to say!) and that you should enjoy using your English to communicate with an English speaker. Most of the exercises in this section are designed to increase your fluency.

Do not worry about how to address the examiner. Use whatever style of address seems appropriate to you (how you talk to your teacher might be a good guide). Listen to the sample interviews on the tape to hear how other candidates talk to the examiner.

It will help if you know the general format of the interview. In all conversations we are, to some extent, anticipating what the other speaker is going to say or ask. This is another important skill: **anticipating content**.

You can prepare yourself for the **type** of question you can expect. Remember not to prepare specific answers. But you will get practice here in all three stages of the interview and this will help you prepare for it. Of course you must also be aware of what the examiner is asking you at any particular time and how you should respond. Listening skills are very important for this.

In the **first** stage of the interview the examiner will ask you some general questions about yourself and the subjects you know about. Some of the questions in the interview will be based on your curriculum vitae. This is a form you fill in when you register for the examination, giving general information about your educational background, work experience and leisure interests. When you go into the interview room, the interviewer will greet you, exchange introductions and then ask you a few basic questions about yourself. This is partly to check the information on the application form and the curriculum vitae but it is also to give you a chance to settle in, relax and warm up.

Exercise 1

With your study partner or group, draw up curricula vitae forms, as below, and fill in your own. Answers do not need to be too detailed.

```
Full name ....................................................................................................
Nationality ..................................................................................................
First language ..............................................................................................
Other languages ...........................................................................................
Educational background ...............................................................................
Occupation and work experience ..................................................................
Study plans ..................................................................................................
Future plans .................................................................................................
Personal interests .........................................................................................
Reason for doing the IELTS test ...................................................................
```

When you have completed your curricula vitae, take turns to: greet each other, introduce yourselves, interview each other to check the information and briefly ask about any unusual or interesting points from the curriculum vitae. These might include your interests, your educational experience, your work, etc.

Time: 2 minutes each.

Having greeted you and checked a few details about you, the examiner will move on to talk about more general topics. The purpose of this, of course, is to get you to talk.

Having chosen a general topic, based on the introduction and/or the curriculum vitae, the examiner will then ask you to say a little more about it. This will often focus on the culture of your country (educational system, social customs, economics, etc.), general related topics, such as city life or your hobbies, or how something you know about is done or what it is like. These are all very broad areas in terms of the number of questions that could be asked and this is another reason why you cannot prepare specific answers.

Get your partner(s) to choose a topic based on your curriculum vitae and to ask you to talk in more detail about it or your opinions of a specific aspect of it. Topics might include work, education, interests such as music and books, some aspect of the culture of your country and the differences between your country and the country you want to study in. Then exchange roles and interview them. Again the most important thing to practise is fluency: try to keep the conversation going.

Time: 3 minutes each.

This exercise is to help you practise giving longer answers. With your partner, make a list of topics, as in exercise 2, and take turns to choose a topic and talk on the subject for 30 seconds without stopping. This is difficult. See which of you can do the best.

Time: 30 seconds per topic.

Discussion

These exercises are all to help you become familiar with the sort of speaking you will have to do in the first stage of the test. Remember to concentrate on fluency and remember to work with your study partner to assess how well you did and to repeat the exercises if necessary.

In the **second stage** of the interview you will be given a simple task for which the interviewer has information you need. You must then ask questions to get that information. You are assessed as to how well you ask those questions. This is the only part of the interview which is not in the form of an ordinary conversation, so it is the only real 'task' you are asked to perform.

In this stage you need to **play a role**. That is, you are given a situation and you have to pretend that you are in it. The purpose of this task, as you know, is to get you to ask questions of the kind you may have to ask when you are in an English speaking country. The interviewer will give you a card with a task on it and a list of things to find out. It is rather like a game. There is nothing to worry about. In fact you have already been doing role-plays in exercises 1 and 2, when you played the role of examiner interviewing your study partner. The next three exercises are role-playing tasks.

The card the interviewer gives you could look like this:

News	
Ask about the news the interviewer has received.	
Find out:	
Details of the news	Interviewer's response
Interviewer's intention	Reason for response

The interviewer will restate the task and invite questions. He or she might say: 'Now I would like you to ask me some questions. I have just received some bad news. Ask me as many different questions as you like, in as many different ways as possible, in order to find out about my news'.

Make sure you are clear about the **purpose** of the task. If you are not sure exactly what you have to do, ask the interviewer to clarify. Here the purpose is to find out as much as you can about the news. Look at the four pieces of information you are asked to find out and think about what questions you need to ask to get them. Be careful not simply to use the words written on the card. They will often be rather formal and in note form; this is not appropriate for spoken English.

Generally when you speak you will need to choose an appropriate way of expressing what you want to say. You should try to express yourself **clearly** and **correctly**. Guidance given in the writing section of this book should also help you when you speak. Look back at the advice given there on organizing your ideas and using correct forms. But remember that spoken English is usually less formal than written English and you will have to think of an **appropriate way** to ask the questions which are given in writing on the task card. For example, for the question about the interviewer's intention it would be unusual (and not very good English) to ask, 'What is your intention?' A more appropriate and natural way of getting information would be to use a less formal question, such as, 'What are you going to do (about it)?'

Exercise 4

Ask your study partner to make up some 'news' for the task above. This might be good news (like a new job) or bad (like illness in the family). They should also work out how they feel about it; what they intend to do; and why. They should not tell you what they have decided. Then role-play the interview. Find out all you can about your study partner's news. Concentrate on appropriate question forms. When you have finished, change roles and let your study partner ask you questions about your 'news'.

Time: 3 to 4 minutes each

Exercise 5

Look at the task below with your study partner(s) and decide together on a topic for the 'report'. Then each of you on your own draw up a timetable, choose your own submission date and change the times you are free. Decide how you want the report to be organized and on the division of the work.

When each of you has all this information, role-play the interview. Choose language appropriate to the situation and pay attention to your question forms.

Meetings

For a class project you must work with the interviewer and produce a joint report. Arrange three meetings to discuss the work.

Find out:

Submission date	Division of the work
Timetable for meetings	Organization of report

You are free every lunchtime except Friday and on Wednesday afternoon.

Time: 3 to 4 minutes.

Exercise 6

Now ask your study partner to take the role of librarian in the task below. They must make notes on the location of the library and other pieces of information which are listed in the task. When they have done this, ask questions to find out more information. Then change roles and let your study partner ask you questions.

Time: 3 to 4 minutes each

Discussion

These exercises are all to help you become familiar with the sort of speaking you will have to do in the second stage. Remember to concentrate on fluency and on using appropriate language. Work with your study partner to assess how well you did. Make up other role-playing exercises if you need more practice at this.

You can learn to use particular **strategies**, such as appropriate expressions, that will help you maintain a well-organized fluent conversation. Some of these phrases will give you time to think. Some of them can get you out of difficulties too! Examples are:

- responding to what has been said: 'That's interesting … ';
  'Yes, I agree … ';
  'I'm not sure I entirely agree … '

- asking for clarification: 'Could you repeat that, please?';
  'Sorry, I don't understand that … ';

- introducing a topic: 'There are two main differences,
  really … ';
  'Well, it's quite simple. First, … ';

- saying you don't know: 'I'm sorry … I'm afraid I don't know
  the answer to that.'

Notice the last expression: IELTS is not designed to assess your knowledge; it is a measure of your competence in English. If you do not know the answer to a question, do not be afraid to say so.

You can make your own list of useful expressions or add to the above. Strategies such as these are the only things worth memorizing for this part of IELTS.

Exercise 7

Add more expressions of your own if you wish and exchange examples with your study partner(s). When your study group has enough examples, test each other on them. Make it into a game. In turn, choose any strategy, for example, asking for clarification. For this, ask: 'What do you say if you don't understand?' If your partner answers correctly, it is their turn to ask you. You may use any of the expressions once only.

In the third stage of the interview you will be asked to talk about your experiences, opinions or future plans. This may mean the immediate future, such as why you have chosen your particular course of study and what you hope to specialize in. You could be asked to describe an aspect of your studies in some detail. Questions could also lead you to talk about your plans for the near future, such as what you hope to do when you graduate. They may also focus on the longer term, less specific future, such as what benefit your studies will be to your country when you return.

There are so many possibilities that it is impossible to predict exactly what questions you will be asked. You can, however, think about probable topic areas. You should also think about the **forms** you will need to answer these questions. These include verb forms such as 'I would like to … ','I hope/plan to … ', 'I am going to … ', 'I may/might … ' as well as time expressions and adverbs like 'possibly', 'probably', etc. Practise these (check the grammar if you need to) but again do not prepare specific answers. As in the earlier sections of the interview, the examiner will change the topic if he or she feels you are giving a prepared answer.

Exercise 8

From the information in the curriculum vitae you prepared for exercise 1, ask each other about your experience and future plans. Ask questions that encourage you to think and give opinions, especially about the future. Use any of the strategies where necessary to give fluent, appropriate answers. At the same time, express your ideas as clearly and accurately as possible.

Time: 3 to 4 minutes each

Having discussed your ideas and future plans the interviewer will conclude the interview. You could ask when you will receive the results but no further questions are expected.

Discussion

As with previous exercises, you and your study partner will have to assess each other and decide whether you need more practice on this topic.

This is the end of the practice section on speaking and the last practice section in this part of the book. Listen to the sample interviews on the cassette which demonstrate the format and stages of the speaking test. Assess for yourself how well the candidates did in giving fluent and appropriate answers.

Continue practising speaking, especially for fluency. Put yourself in situations where you need to speak English. Practise asking questions and practise talking about the sort of topics mentioned above. Pay attention to accuracy too. If you have particular problems with grammar or pronunciation consult one of the books in the bibliography.

Summary

What you need to **know**
How to talk fluently
How to anticipate content
How to use appropriate language
How to use strategies

Here are some points to remember:

1   The format of the test is as follows:

In the **first** section of the interview you will be asked questions about **yourself** and **general topics**.

In the **second** section you find information that you need in a particular situation by **asking questions**.

In the **last** section you will be asked questions about your **opinions, studies** and **future plans**.

2   Try to talk as much and as fluently as possible. Do not let concern about accuracy obstruct fluency.

3   Do not prepare specific answers: they will not be useful and they will make it more difficult for you to do a good interview.

4   Relax, be confident and enjoy using your English.

Finally, if you want to run through the whole IELTS examination as a final preparation you should get a copy of the IELTS *specimen materials*, which are available from your local test centre.

Section two: further practice

Introduction

This section contains extra practice materials to help you prepare for the reading and writing subtests. It is divided into two parts. First there are four full-length reading and writing papers. These are followed by a supplementary section containing additional writing tests. Answers to the reading questions are in the answer key. All questions are timed, and length, topics, level of difficulty, format and question types are similar to what you can expect in the examination itself.

Instructions and time limits are given in the exercises. When you work through them you should make sure that you:

- follow the instructions carefully;

- keep to the time limit;

- do **not** consult the answer key until you have completed the exercise.

You will need paper on which to write your answers. For reading questions this answer sheet should have numbered spaces or boxes for your answers.

Paper 1

Reading passage

You are advised to spend about 20 minutes on the questions based on this reading passage.

Job satisfaction and personnel mobility

Europe, and indeed all the major industrialized nations, is currently going through a recession. This obviously has serious implications for companies and personnel who find themselves victims of the downturn. As Britain apparently eases out of recession, there are also potentially equally serious implications for the companies who survive, associated with the employment and recruitment market in general.

During a recession, voluntary staff turnover is bound to fall sharply. Staff who have been with a company for some years will clearly not want to risk losing their accumulated redundancy rights. Furthermore, they will be unwilling to go to a new organization where they may well be joining on a 'last in, first out' basis. Consequently, even if there is little or no job satisfaction in their current post, they are most likely to remain where they are, quietly sitting it out and waiting for things to improve. In Britain, this situation has been aggravated by the length and nature of the recession – as may also prove to be the case in the rest of Europe and beyond.

In the past, companies used to take on staff at the lower levels and reward loyal employees with internal promotions. This opportunity for a lifetime career with one company is no longer available, owing to 'downsizing' of companies, structural reorganizations and redundancy programmes, all of which have affected middle management as much as the lower levels. This reduction in the layers of management has led to flatter hierarchies, which, in turn, has reduced promotion prospects within most companies. Whereas ambitious personnel had become used to regular promotion, they now find their progress is blocked.

This situation is compounded by yet another factor. When staff at any level are taken on, it is usually from outside and promotion is increasingly through career moves between companies. Recession has created a new breed of bright young graduates, much more self-interested and cynical than in the past. They tend to be more wary, sceptical of what is on offer and consequently much tougher negotiators. Those who joined companies directly from education feel the effects most strongly and now feel uncertain and insecure in mid-life.

In many cases, this has resulted in staff dissatisfaction. Moreover, management itself has contributed to this general ill-feeling and frustration. The caring image of the recent past has gone and the fear of redundancy is often used as the prime motivator.

As a result of all these factors, when the recession eases and people find more confidence, there will be an explosion of employees seeking new opportunities to escape their current jobs. This will be led by younger, less-experienced employees and the hard-headed young graduates. 'Headhunters' confirm that older staff are still cautious, having seen so many good companies 'go to the wall', and are reluctant to jeopardize their redundancy entitlements. Past experience, however, suggests that, once triggered, the expansion in recruitment will be very rapid.

The problem which faces many organizations is one of strategic planning; of not knowing who will leave and who will stay. Often it is the best personnel who move on whilst the worst cling to the little security they have. This is clearly a problem for companies, who need a stable core on which to build strategies for future growth.

Whilst this expansion in the recruitment market is likely to happen soon in Britain, most employers are simply not prepared. With the loss of middle management, in a static marketplace, personnel management and recruitment are often conducted by junior personnel. They have only known recession and lack the experience to plan ahead and to implement strategies for growth. This is true of many other functions, leaving companies without the skills, ability or vision to structure themselves for long-term growth. Without this ability to recruit competitively for strategic planning, and given the speed at which these changes are likely to occur, a real crisis seems imminent.

Questions 1–2

According to the information in the reading passage, select the most appropriate of the given options (A–D). Write the appropriate letter for each question in boxes 1–2 on your answer sheet.

1   The current economic downturn …

A   has serious consequences for personnel and companies which survive

B   has serious consequences for companies which survive

C   may have serious consequences for companies which survive

D   has serious consequences for voluntary staff

2   Many staff are not leaving their jobs because …

A   they will lose their redundancy rights

B   they would join a new company on a 'last in, first out' basis

C   they are waiting for the economy to pick up

D   they are dissatisfied with their current position

Questions 3–8

In questions 3–8, complete each sentence by choosing one of the possible endings from the list below, which best reflects the information in the reading passage. Write the corresponding letter (A–K) for each question in boxes 3–8 on your answer sheet. Note there are more choices than spaces, so you will not need to use all of them.

The first one has been done for you as an example.

Example	*Answer*
A lifetime career with one company …	E

3   The 'downsizing' of companies …

4   Ambitious personnel …

5   Today, new graduates …

6   Long-serving personnel …

7   Management policy …

8   Companies often care less about staff and …

List of possible endings

A   has often contributed to staff dissatisfaction

B   are more sceptical and less trusting

C   has affected all levels of personnel

D   use fear as a means of motivation

E   was usual in the past

F   career moves between companies

G   reduce the layers of management

H   feel uncertain and insecure

I   increasingly have to look elsewhere for promotion

J   is a result of flatter hierarchies

K   reward loyal employees with internal promotions

Questions 9–13

The paragraph below is a summary of the last section of the reading passage. Complete the summary by choosing *no more than two words* from the reading passage to fill each space. Write your answers in boxes 9–13 on your answer sheet.

Example	*Answer*
Taking all of these various …	factors
into consideration	

when the economy picks up and people … **9** …, there will be a very rapid expansion in recruitment. Younger employees and graduates will lead the search for new jobs, older staff being more … **10** … Not knowing who will leave creates a problem for companies; they need a … **11** … of personnel to plan and build future strategies. This is a serious matter, as … **12** … is often conducted by inexperienced staff, owing to the loss of many middle management positions. This inability to recruit strategically will leave many companies without the skills and vision to plan ahead and … **13** … to achieve long term growth.

Question 14

In your view, is the writer of the reading passage warning the reader about a coming …

A   economic crisis

B   personnel management crisis

C   redundancy crisis?

    Write the appropriate letter (A–C) in box 14 on your answer sheet.

Reading passage

You are advised to spend about 20 minutes on the questions based on this reading passage.

The education gap

Education is the passport to modern life, and a pre-condition of national prosperity. But more than a quarter of the world's adults – 900 million – cannot read or write, and more than 100 million young children are deprived of even a primary school education. In most developing countries, after decades of educational expansion, spending on learning is falling. The illiterate are virtually helpless in a world ruled by the written word, where notices and official papers can seem a mass of meaningless hieroglyphics. People who cannot decipher them are at the mercy of those who can; many, as a result, have been cheated of their rights or their land.

Studies show that people with even a basic education are healthier and eat better. They are more likely to plan their families and their children are more likely to survive. According to the World Bank, just four years of primary education enables farmers to increase productivity by ten per cent, often the difference between hunger and sufficiency. National economic returns from education outstrip those from most other forms of investment.

Enrolment: rise and fall

As they became independent, most developing countries enthusiastically embraced education. Two decades of astonishing expansion followed. Between 1960 and 1981, the world's thirty-two poorest countries (excluding India and China, which have long had good records) increased the proportion of their children enrolled in primary school from thirty-eight to seventy-two per cent. The thirty-eight next poorest achieved almost universal primary school enrolment by 1980; up from about two-thirds in 1960. It seemed as if it would not be long before every child alive could be sure of going to school.

By the end of the 1980s, that dream had turned to bitter disillusion. The decade brought economic disaster to developing countries. They slumped when rich nations went into recession at the beginning of the 1980s, the subsequent recovery passed them by and they were hit again by the renewed recession in the late 1980s and early 1990s. The educational expansion of the 1960s and 1970s first halted, then went into reverse. By 1989, enrolment rates had dropped in one out of every five developing countries. In some African countries, the number of children in primary schools declined by a third between 1980 and 1985. Tanzania's universal primary school enrolment fell to less than seventy-five per cent. Unesco's Director-General, Federico Mayor, warns that this threatens to 'set back the countries of the South by a whole generation or even more'.

Declining expenditure

The proportion of national expenditure going to education declined in more than half of developing countries over the 1980s. In the world's thirty-seven poorest countries, the average expenditure per head on education dropped by a quarter. In Africa as a whole, says the World Bank, only $0.60 a year is spent on educational materials for each student, whilst it estimates 'minimum requirements' at $5.00.

Illiteracy and the poor

In industrialized countries, absolute illiteracy was largely eradicated half a century ago; they contain only two per cent of the world's illiterate. 'Functional illiteracy', however, remains: in Canada, the literacy of a quarter of all adults is seriously inadequate; in the

United States, estimates range from five to twenty-five per cent; in France, the total numbers range from two to eight million people, depending on the study. Most are among the poorest members of their societies.

Generally speaking, the poorer a country, the higher the number of illiterate; two-thirds of adults in the very poorest countries cannot read or write. Furthermore, the poorest individuals suffer most. The poorer a child's family, the less likely he (or, particularly, she) is to start school and the more likely it is that those who do start will drop out.

The disadvantaged countryside

More people in the Third World live in the countryside, where schools and teachers are always scarcer. But even in the cities, the poor miss out. In Calcutta, over sixty per cent of children do not attend school because they have to work to help keep the family going, or look after younger siblings to enable their mothers to work. Two-thirds of the children who either never start school or drop out early, are girls. Two-thirds of the world's illiterate are women. Yet women's education is particularly important. The World Bank identifies it as 'perhaps the single most important determinant of family health and nutrition', and its research shows that infant mortality rates fall steadily, and dramatically, for every year women spend at school. But tradition, prejudices and the burden of work to be done at home ensure that daughters are pulled out of school first. In the first grade of Kampala's primary schools, the sexes are evenly balanced; by the seventh grade, there are more than twice as many boys as girls.

Primary education: the productive dollar

Every dollar invested in primary school education, according to another World Bank study, is fifty per cent more productive than one invested in secondary schooling, and gives twice as much as one spent on universities. Yet, throughout the Third World, these spending priorities are reversed.

A few countries have started to change their priorities, emphasizing primary education. Zimbabwe doubled its number of primary schools in its first five years of independence; the proportion of its budget spent on education is the fifth highest in the world, and the curriculum has been re-orientated to meet local needs. Bangladesh has opened more than 2,500 basic village primary schools with appropriate syllabuses since 1985, at an annual cost of just $15.00 per pupil. Only 1.5 per cent of the children drop out, compared to sixty per cent of their peers in the ordinary primary schools. Moreover, ninety-five per cent of pupils, the majority girls, continue their education after leaving.

Nonetheless, all these countries are under harsh economic pressure. There is little hope for the children of the Third World countries, even if their governments do change their priorities, unless their countries are enabled to develop.

Questions 15–16

15 What are the two most important benefits of education given by the writer of the reading passage?

Write your answer in box 15 on your answer sheet.

16 What do you think is the main purpose of the passage?

A   to promote the development of primary education

B   to promote the development of tertiary education

C   to illustrate the need for development in general

D   to highlight the problems of rural areas

Write the appropriate letter (A–D) in box 16 on your answer sheet.

Questions 17–21

For questions 17–21, complete the table below by selecting the most appropriate answer from the list beneath the table. Write the corresponding letter (A–J) in boxes 17–21 on your answer sheet.

	1960	1980 1981	1985	1989
Enrolment	*Example* 32 poorest countries	*Answer* J		
	38 next poorest	17		
	18		19	
Expenditure	20		21	

List of possible answers

A   Tanzania

B   India and China

C   the thirty-seven poorest countries

D   some African countries

E   decreased by a quarter

F   decreased by over a quarter

G   decreased by a third

H   decreased by a half

I   increased to nearly 100%

J   increased from thirty-eight per cent to seventy-two per cent

Questions 22–25

In questions 22–25, choose which of the answers best represents the information in the reading passage. Write the appropriate letter (A–D) for each question in boxes 22–25 on your answer sheet.

Example   *Answer*

A basic education for women …   A

A   can determine the health and nutrition of the family

B   makes the difference between hunger and sufficiency

C   only lasts for four years

D   increases productivity by ten per cent

22   Illiteracy has been almost completely eradicated …

A   from the developing world

B   except in the USA, Canada and France

C   in absolute terms in industrialized countries.

D   in functional terms in industrialized countries

23 Girls very often fail to complete their schooling because ...

A   they have to go out to work

B   there are twice as many boys as girls

C   of tradition and prejudice

D   of family health and nutrition

24 Spending on tertiary education is ...

A   twice as productive as spending on secondary education

B   only half as productive as spending on primary education

C   fifty per cent less productive than spending on secondary schooling

D   twenty-five per cent less productive than spending on primary schooling

25 Primary education has been given more importance ...

A   in Calcutta

B   in some parts of Africa and Asia

C   in the last five years

D   by reorienting the curriculum

Reading passage

You are advised to spend about 20 minutes on the questions based on the reading passage below.

Developing environmental management strategies

Strong and sustainable economic activity depends on healthy environmental management. It is being increasingly recognized by the public, government and industry that there is a need to shift smoothly from a 'react and cure' approach to an 'anticipate and prevent' approach. The mechanism governing this change started to appear three to four years ago and the momentum for change has been gathering steadily ever since.

Whilst the need to embrace these changes is almost universally accepted, the mechanisms for change and the priorities for action have been far from clear. The public and the media point to anecdotal evidence of lack of progress or setbacks, over a bewildering range of topics. These incidents are catalogued by local and national pressure groups to enhance their own campaigns for change. The Government, under pressure from the European Community, has introduced legislation which, although progressive, often appears to industry to be fragmented and difficult to digest.

There is, therefore, a clear and often expressed need on the part of British and European management for techniques to identify and prioritize the key environmental issues for allocation of resources and action. The technique emerging as the most effective is a strategy which involves the formulation of a policy statement setting out the organization's philosophy on the environment and the aims to be achieved. A detailed assessment of the environmental status and performance of the operation is then undertaken, key issues identified and targets set. The performance of the operation or unit is regularly audited to measure progress towards the targets set. This environmental strategy is often called an Environmental Management System or simply referred to as an Environmental Audit.

The need for environmental strategies

Over the past few years, the incentives for introducing such an Environmental Risk Management Strategy have changed as public attitude has evolved, insurance markets have hardened and national legislation has been enacted. Environmental Risk Management Strategies may therefore be implemented for reasons of insurance, market forces, acquisitions, national legislation or Environmental Accreditation Schemes.

The basic elements of the Environmental Strategies currently being proposed by most authorities are as follows:

Environmental strategy

An Environmental Strategy is a documented plan, comprising the drawing up of an Environmental Policy and an Initial Environmental Assessment, which provides prioritized recommendations for action and targets to be achieved. This is followed by regular audits to measure progress towards the targets.

Environmental policy

An Environmental Policy is a statement of the overall aims and principles of action of an organization with respect to the environment. It may be expressed in general terms, but it may also include quantitative targets.

Initial environmental assessment

An Initial Environmental Assessment is a comprehensive assessment of the environmental impact as a result of an organization's activities. It leads to a report to top management in which the key issues are identified and priorities for action allocated. This initial Environmental Assessment is referred to in the Draft British Standard as an Environmental Effects Inventory and in the Draft Eco-Audit scheme as an Environmental Review. The topics covered in Initial Assessments may include a review of management systems, a historical review of the site, assessment of emissions and impact on air, water and land as well as control and monitoring of emissions. Noise, odours, recycling, disposal and duty of care will usually come into the assessment, as will raw materials management, savings, transportation, storage, water conservation, energy management and products planning. Other important aspects of the assessment are the prevention and mitigation of accidents, unexpected and foreseen pollution and of course staff information, the relationship with the public and the need for Environmental Audits.

An Environmental Audit is systematic, documented, periodic and an objective evaluation of how well the organization's systems are performing, assessed against internal procedures and compliance with internal policies and statutory requirements.

Both the Draft British Standard and Draft Eco-Audit scheme stipulate that the audits should be carried out by personnel independent of the plant or process being audited.

Environmental statements

Under the UK Environmental Protection Act the details declared in the application for Authorization to Operate are included in a Register which is open to the public. Such legislation also exists in many of the other European Community countries.

The Eco-Audit scheme also proposes that organizations which are accredited under the scheme should regularly publish an environmental statement containing factual information and data on the environmental performance of each site.

Questions 26–28

Read the following statements and say how they reflect the information in the reading passage by writing:

T   if it is true according to the passage,

F   if it is false according to the passage, and

II   if there is insufficient information in the passage.

　　Write your answers in boxes 26–28 on your answer sheet.

　　The first one has been done as an example.

Example　　　　　　　　　　　　　　　　　　*Answer*

A 'react and cure' policy is replacing　　　　F

the 'anticipate and prevent' approach

to environmental management.

26　European Community directives on environmental management are clear and easily implemented.

27　Allocation of resources within companies for action on environmental issues is governed by legislation.

28　An organization's philosophy and aims with respect to the environment are stated in its Environmental Policy.

Questions 29–34

The paragraph below is a summary of the first part of the reading passage. Complete the summary by choosing one or two words from the reading passage to complete the spaces 29–34. Write the words in boxes 29–34 on your answer sheet.

　　The first one has been done for you as an example.

Summary: Developing environmental management strategies

Example　　　　　　　　　　　　　　　　　　*Answer*

There has been a steady movement

towards more efficient, proactive …　　　　environmental management

Whilst the … **29** … is generally accepted, the means have yet to be agreed. Attempts at introducing … **30** … have, so far, been ineffective. Techniques are currently being defined for allocating … **31** … to act on key environmental issues. Policies are formulated, detailed assessments conducted and performance measured. These evaluations, or … **32** …, are carried out objectively by … **33** … personnel and … **34** … against both internal and external criteria.

Questions 35–37

Read the following statements and say how they reflect the information in the reading passage, by writing:

C   if it is correct according to the passage,

I   if it is incorrect according to the passage, and

NC   if it is not clear from the information in the passage.

Write your answers in boxes 35–37 on your answer sheet.

35 All EC countries have an environmental register which is open to the public.

36 The Eco-Audit Scheme insists that members publish data on performance.

37 Environmental information is kept at each of a company's sites.

Questions 38–40

38 Give three factors which have been responsible for increasing interest in Environmental Risk Management.

Write *two words for each factor* in box 38 on your answer sheet.

39 State the four characteristics of an Environmental Audit which are mentioned in the passage.

Write a *maximum of five words* in box 39 on your answer sheet.

40 According to the information in the package, Eco-Audit accredited organizations should publish quarterly statements.

Is this:

i   true;

ii   information not given;

iii   false?

Write the appropriate numeral (i – iii) in box 40 on your answer sheet.

Writing task 1

You should spend no more than 20 minutes on this task.

Look at the figures for expenditure on education in figure 6 below.

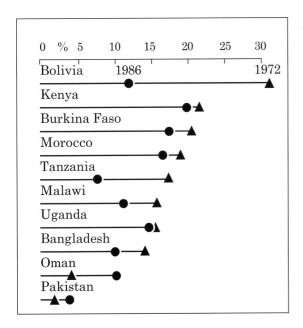

Figure 6 Spending on education as % of total government expenditure in selected developing countries

Task:

Using the information on the countries in figure 6 above, describe the changes in the levels of spending on education, in general terms and with specific examples.

You should write at least 150 words.

Writing task 2

You should spend no more than 40 minutes on this task.

Task:

People can no longer expect a job for life. What should individuals and governments do to prepare the current and future environments for different working conditions?

You should write at least 250 words.

You may use ideas from the reading passage. You should use your own ideas and experience and support your argument with examples.

Do *not* copy directly from the reading passage.

Paper 2

Reading passage

You are advised to spend about 20 minutes on the questions based on the reading passage below.

Birth of a profession

As pressure grows on companies to respond to environmental issues, one of the easiest ways to do so is to appoint an environmental manager from inside the organization, whether or not they already have a quality or health and safety manager or director. It is another matter whether or not it makes any difference to the environmental performance of that company.

It is in response to the needs of these personnel, thrust suddenly into an entirely new role in the corporate structure, that an initiative was launched a year ago to provide a framework of key standards of competence. It is nearing its closing stage of development but that will then lead on to further phases in creating what is intended to be a new breed of professional, capable of wielding the same authority as his or her colleagues inside the company.

The Institute of Environmental Managers was established last year to create a forum for those often in a still embryonic role to learn and exchange methods, rather than struggle in isolation with what their companies increasingly demand of them. The Institute's members, now numbering about 400, range from some of those in large multi-nationals, who have been developing expertise and experience over a number of years, to newcomers in the field, often in smaller organizations. Concern that many were struggling in the deep end was confirmed in a survey, carried out by the Institute on its members, on the stature of the environmental managers in the UK.

The co-director of the Centre for Environment and Business in Scotland, which provides the secretariat for the Institute, explained that these managers were looking for some sort of support. The main problem was the attitude of other people in the company, both of the management and of the workforce, resulting in slipping priorities and difficulties in gaining access to the decision makers.

A principal factor that was identified was that there was no formal recognition of individuals' environmental management skills and, indeed, that they had no standards of competence to aim for. One of the first things the Institute's steering group, which oversees its day-to-day matters, therefore decided to do was to establish these. After much brainstorming and interviews with environmental managers, six key areas of competence were defined: strategic vision; business awareness; management skills; motivation, training and leadership; external communications; and crisis management.

The management element has been specified very strongly because a lot of environ-mental managers, although technically very competent people, are being pushed into a management role with very few of the required skills. On the other hand, some experience of their organization will remain a prerequisite, as the managers have to be aware of their own business and how it works. People who have come straight out of university having studied environmental management will be of little use, so the environmental remit is being given to people who are already well-established in the company, probably in middle management. While some big companies may want to train their own specialist team of managers straight from university, this situation is unlikely to change dramatically.

While all decision-makers round the company will be responsible for their own areas, the environmental manager will act as co-ordinator, providing the framework. To standardize the levels of competence for such a multi-disciplinary role, to be taken up by people from different career routes, education and training will become a matter of complementing and extending individuals' own knowledge and expertise.

A survey of training in Scotland is currently being conducted to establish what kind of courses are provided and whether they are suitable for business people who have insufficient time to do a modular course. A similar project is under way for the rest of the UK, identifying centres of excellence on a regional basis, so that people know they can go to at least one centre near them. The long-term plan is to work with educational establishments to design courses in line with required competences, so providing the business community with the training it requires on a flexible, modular basis. In the meantime, with the final consultation period for the standards and assessment procedure completed, the aim is to start inviting applicants to put themselves forward for assessment leading to full membership.

The Institute is confident there is demand, both from managers and their employers. The aim is to empower the environmental managers and to get them professional status, so they start being considered seriously within their companies. The growing need to be able to demonstrate this commitment through certification, and other needs, will only add to this demand.

The environmental management systems standard BS7750 in its final draft stipulates that 'the organization shall appoint a management representative who, irrespective of other responsibilities, shall have defined authority and responsibility for ensuring that the requirements of this standard are implemented and maintained'. More and more companies, however, will look beyond even this. The intention, then, is to produce a code of practice for members, to enable them to say to their employers, in difficult situations, that they have professional standards to maintain and must be taken seriously.

Far from being confrontational, the belief is that companies will become aware of the importance of having, and indeed spotlighting, someone responsible for managing their environmental policy. It will provide their customers, financiers, insurers and regulators with greater assurance than simply demonstrating compliance.

Questions 1–9

The paragraph below is a summary of the reading passage. Complete the summary by choosing *no more than three words* from the reading passage to fill the spaces numbered 1–9. Write the words in boxes 1–9 on your answer sheet.

The first one has been done for you as an example.

Summary: Birth of a profession

Example	*Answer*
One way for companies to respond to	
pressure on environmental issues is to …	appoint
an environmental manager.	

These ... **1** ..., however, need a framework of key standards of competence before they will be regarded as professionals. The Institute of Environmental Managers was established to fulfil this need by drawing together isolated individuals, some experienced within ... **2** ..., other newcomers from smaller organizations, thus providing an opportunity to exchange ideas. Many need this support, as prevailing attitudes make it difficult to gain access to decision-makers. The aim is to establish much needed ... **3** ..., to gain ... **4** ... of environmental management skills and to achieve professional status through certification. Management skills are emphasized, as environmental management is a ... **5** ..., co-ordinating role where both knowledge and expertise are necessary. Training will thus need to extend the skills of experienced individuals from differing backgrounds. The Centre aims to identify regional ... **6** ... and provide relevant, ... **7** ... courses and to establish a ... **8** ... to support members. Companies should also welcome this move as they become increasingly aware of ... **9** ... taking environmental matters seriously.

Questions 10–14

The list below contains six descriptions or definitions of the key areas defined in the reading passage. Match each description or definition with the relevant area of competence.

Write your answers in boxes 10–14 on your answer sheet.

Example   *Answer*

to understand the need for an emergency

action plan and be able to justify the

contingency measures   crisis management

10 to ensure environmental measures are effectively communicated to and adopted by others

11 to identify cost-efficient solutions in a commercial context

12 to handle individuals and organizations outside

13 to undertake effective project and systems management and internal communications

14 to see beyond strict compliance and steer the company towards a sustainable future

Questions 15–16

15 Most big companies will prefer to take graduates straight out of university.

Write either *true* or *false* in box 15 on your answer sheet.

16 400 applicants have put themselves forward for assessment.

Write either *true* or *false* in box 16 on your answer sheet.

Reading passage

You are advised to spend about 25 minutes on the questions based on this reading passage.

Rethinking Europe: ICI and the Single European Market

Recently, amid a fanfare of proclamations by its senior managers about the need to 'reshape for the single market challenge', the world's fourth largest chemical multi-national created a new regional organization, based in Brussels. Then, barely sixteen months later, it decided quietly – although amid internal controversy – to shut it down. The closing down of ICI Europe, in the countryside near Brussels, reflects the company's new-found willingness to adjust to changing circumstances far more rapidly than in the past.

By reversing its decision, ICI had done two things. First, it recognized that it had overrated the potential demand from multi-national customers – ranging from BMW to several household appliance makers – for cross-border European sales co-ordination across its various businesses. Instead, it now feels that any pan-European sales 'synergies' can be handled within individual businesses. Second, the turnaround represented the final triumph within ICI of a movement which, as in many multi-nationals today, was already on the rise inside the chemical company before the Brussels decision was taken: the need to speed decision-making and cut costs by streamlining the complex 'matrix' structures through which they had been managed since the 1960s.

In September 1990, when ICI celebrated the opening of ICI Europe, a clear shift of influence towards the global businesses, away from its existing regional organizations and national companies, had already been under way since the 1970s. Although the reasons for the creation of ICI Europe seemed powerful to those directly involved and to the outside world, it was seen elsewhere within ICI as being inappropriately timed.

With hindsight, it is said that ICI Europe was really a project, not a permanent organization. This is because its most publicized purpose, the creation of 'corporate coherence' towards customers in continental Europe, proved to be ahead of its time. Car companies, for instance, still prefer not to purchase through a single point, even if four ICI businesses supply them separately with paint, polyurethane for bumpers, advanced materials for engines, and fibres for seats.

ICI is by no means the only large multi-national which, in its Euro-enthusiasm, misread its customers' purchasing intentions in this way. Nonetheless, it is surprising that ICI accepted the now mainly discredited 'supermarket' theory of business-to-business purchasing. The result was that ICI Europe's main tasks from the start actually turned out to be transitional:

- *To establish an orderly transfer of sales activities and staff from the fifteen national companies to ICI's global businesses, splitting sales staff into European sub-regions such as Benelux, Nordic and what ICI calls 'mid-Europe' (Germany, Austria and Switzerland).*

- *To support the businesses across Europe by creating half a dozen sub-regional centres for shared 'support services', such as information technology, finance, health and safety, public affairs and personnel.*

- *To streamline the old way of maintaining a 'corporate presence' in each country.*

By the summer of 1991, several things had happened:

- *Most of the first two tasks were well in hand or complete.*

- *The business climate had changed for the worse, and ICI's profits had slumped. Moreover, a takeover was threatened and a desperate hunt was under way within ICI to simplify structures and cut costs.*

- *From the beginning of 1991 the group's fourteen businesses had been agglomerated into eight larger units, all with revenues of more than £1 billion. If necessary, regional co-ordination could be done at that level.*

- *It was felt that the upkeep of ICI Europe was affecting their European selling costs. Furthermore, it was also felt that control over the entire business process, from the customer right back to the factory, was being affected.*

The response from ICI's top management was to set up a study group. It decided that ICI Europe had, in effect, fulfilled much of its remit. It should be shut down, and its remaining activities split up. The provision of shared services would be transferred to the strongest business in each country or sub-region. At the same time a senior manager in each business would be selected to act as a part-time 'ICI supremo' there. The first to take on such a representative role, for the whole Nordic area, was the head of ICI Pharmaceuticals.

Both these moves follow the growing tendency within other multi-nationals of streamlining their bureaucracies, by delegating such geographic 'head office' responsibilities to senior divisional managers on a part-time basis. The decision to conform with international practice was not unanimous, however. There were complaints that it was not adequately discussed and it was opposed by the main ICI board member responsible for Europe, by the chairman of ICI Europe, and by one of the business heads. One concern was that ICI might lose continental perspective; another was that it would lose the ability to develop international managers capable of moving across businesses.

The costs saved by shutting ICI Europe are hard to estimate, since about twenty of its sixty staff have been transferred, either to the UK head office or to the businesses. More significantly, its efforts cut the cost of ICI's continental support services by a fifth between 1990 and 1992. There is potentially at least as much again to be saved through streamlining within the businesses.

Questions 17–19

Complete each sentence below with a *maximum of three words* from the reading passage. Write your answers in boxes 17–19 on your answer sheet.

Example	*Answer*
ICI was attempting to prepare for …	the single market

17   One of the main reasons that ICI reversed its decision was that it had …

18   One purpose of streamlining company structures is to …

19   Another purpose is …

Questions 20–21

In questions 20–21, choose which of the options best represents the information in the reading passage. Write the appropriate letter (A–D) for each question in boxes 20–21 on your answer sheet.

20 Its planned 'corporate coherence' failed because ICI …

A   bought discredited supermarkets

B   misread customers' purchasing power

C   misjudged customers' purchasing plans

D   discredited business-to-business purchasing

21 ICI's main tasks were to …

A   transfer, streamline and support operations

B   support its services, such as information technology

C   form fifteen national companies

D   transfer sales and services to mid-Europe

Questions 22–29

The paragraph below is a summary of the middle section of the reading passage. Complete the summary by choosing the appropriate word, phrase of clause from the list below to fill the spaces numbered 22–29. Write the corresponding letter (A–N) in boxes 22–29 on your answer sheet. There are more choices than spaces, so you will not need to use all of them.

The first one has been done for you as an example.

Summary: Rethinking Europe

Example	*Answer*
After a year most staff had been transferred to the … and support service centres had been created.	E

Owing to the … **22** …, however, profits … **23** … and a take-over was threatened. This forced … **24** … on streamlining the business. Eight units, each with a revenue … **25** …. £1 billion, had been formed and it was decided that regional co-ordination could be achieved at that level. Nonetheless, it was still felt that … **26** … ICI Europe was not cost-effective and that there had been a … **27** … over the entire production to after-sales process. A study group was established, which decided, on the basis of what had been accomplished, to close ICI Europe, transfer the shared service centres to one business … **28** … and to appoint a senior manager there to act as … **29** … on a part-time basis.

List of possible answers

A   further action

B   were down substantially

C   worsening economic situation

D   marked economic situation

E   sub-regions

F   corporate coherence

G   loss of control

H   maintaining

I   representative

J   the upkeep

K   in excess of

L   in each area

M   in each country

N   a desperate search

Questions 30–32

30   Did the study group feel that ICI Europe had been a *partial success* or a *total failure*?

Write *one of the given phrases* in box 30 on your answer sheet.

31   How many people opposed the study group's decision?

Write a *number* in box 31 on your answer sheet.

32   How much more could be saved on continental support service costs?

Write *words or figures* in box 32 on your answer sheet.

Reading passage

You are advised to spend about 15 minutes on the questions based on the reading passage below.

The muddle of MBAs[1]

It is incongruous that the number of British institutions offering MBA courses should have grown by 254 per cent during a period when the economy has been sliding into deeper recession. Optimists, or those given to speedy assumptions, might think it marvellous to have such a resource of business school graduates ready for the recovery. Unfortunately, there is now much doubt about the value of the degree – not least among MBA graduates themselves, suffering as they are from the effects of recession and facing the prospect of shrinking management structures.

What was taken some years ago as a ticket of certain admission to success is now being exposed to the scrutiny of cost-conscious employers who seek 'can-dos' rather than 'might-dos', and who feel that academia has not been sufficiently appreciative of the needs of industry or of the employers' possible contribution.

It is curious, given the name of the degree, that there should be no league table for UK business schools; no unanimity about what the degree should encompass; and no agreed system of accreditation. Surely there is something wrong. One wonders where all the tutors for this massive infusion of business expertise came from and why all this mushrooming took place.

Perhaps companies that made large investments would have been wiser to invest in already existing managers, perched anxiously on their own internal ladders. The Institute of Management's 1992 survey, which revealed that eighty-one per cent of managers thought they would be more effective if they received more training, suggests that this might be the case. There is, too, the fact that training alone does not make successful managers. They need the inherent qualifications of character; a degree of self-subjugation; and, above all, the ability to communicate and lead; more so now, when empowerment is a buzzword that is at least generating genuflexions, if not total conviction.

One can easily think of people, some comparatively unlettered, who are now lauded captains of industry. We may, therefore, not need to be too concerned about the fall in applications for business school places, or even the doubt about MBAs. The proliferation and subsequent questioning may have been an inevitable evolution. If the Management Charter Initiative, now exploring the introduction of a senior management qualification, is successful, there will be a powerful corrective.

We believe now that management is all about change. One hopes there will be some of that in the relationship between management and science within industry, currently causing concern and which is overdue for attention. No-one doubts that we need more scientists and innovation to give us an edge in an increasingly competitive world. If scientists feel themselves undervalued and under-used, working in industrial ghettos, that is not a promising augury for the future. It seems we have to resolve these misapprehensions between science and industry. Above all, we have to make sure that management is not itself smug about its status and that it does not issue mission statements about communication without realising that the essence of it is a dialogue. More empowerment is required – and we should strive to achieve it.

[1] Master of Business Administration

Questions 33–36

In questions 33–36, choose which of the answers (A–D) best represents the information in the reading passage. Write the appropriate letter (A–D) for each question in boxes 33–36 on your answer sheet.

33 What is the writer's view in the reading passage? He believes that …

A   there are too many MBAs

B   the degree is over-valued

C   standards are inconsistent

D   the degree has dubious value

34 According to the passage, employers …

A   feel that they have not been consulted sufficiently about their needs

B   consider that cost-consciousness is the most important qualification

C   are more concerned about the value of the degree than graduates themselves

D   feel that MBAs will not be necessary because of shrinking management structures

35 According to the passage, …

A   managers need a degree and the ability to communicate

B   training needs to be done in groups to be successful

C   managers today must have good communication and leadership skills

D   industrial managers do not need to write letters

36 In the writer's opinion, …

A   science increases competition

B   scientists are undervalued

C   the management of science needs reassessment

D   management feels smug about its status

Questions 37–40

Read the following statements and say how they reflect the information in the reading passage, by writing:

A   if you agree with the statement;

D   if you disagree with the statement;

U   if the information is not clearly given in the passage.

Write your answers in boxes 37–40 on your answer sheet.

The first one has been done for you as an example.

Example	*Answer*
The number of MBA courses being offered more than doubled during the recession.	A

37   Employers today are looking for proven experience rather than potential ability.

38   Most managers interviewed felt that their colleagues needed more training.

39   The Management Charter Initiative is an attempt to standardize MBAs.

40   Companies would have benefited more from investing in their own staff rather than recruiting MBAs.

Writing task 1

You should spend no more than 20 minutes on this task.

Study the data in figure 7 below, showing the factors which have influenced decision-makers on environmental policy, as obtained by telephone interviews.

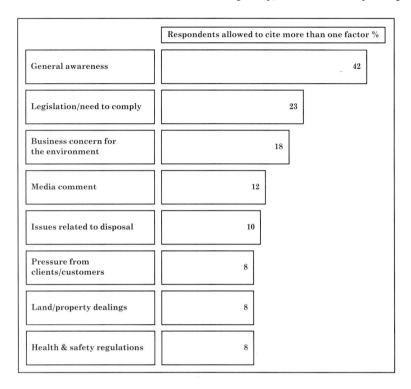

	Respondents allowed to cite more than one factor %
General awareness	42
Legislation/need to comply	23
Business concern for the environment	18
Media comment	12
Issues related to disposal	10
Pressure from clients/customers	8
Land/property dealings	8
Health & safety regulations	8

Figure 7 Factors which prompted consideration of environmental issues

Task:

Describe the pattern of responses.

You should write at least 150 words.

Writing task 2

You should spend no more than 40 minutes on this task

Task:

Write a short essay for a university lecturer, arguing either for or against the following proposition:

As technological innovation brings about rapid changes and retraining becomes a lifelong necessity, industry should take over more and more of the responsibility for education.

You should write at least 250 words.

You should use your own ideas and experience and support your argument with relevant examples.

Paper 3

You are advised to spend about 20 minutes on questions 1–16 based on the reading passage below.

Questions 1–5

The reading passage *NVQs in retailing – the BHS experience* has six sections. Choose the most suitable heading for each section from the list below (A–L) and write the corresponding letter in boxes 1–5 on your answer sheet. Note there are more headings than sections, so you will not need to use all of them. You may use the same heading for more than one answer if you wish.

List of headings

A   The Storehouse Group

B   Putting theory into practice

C   Cause for the initiative

D   Increased dividends

E   Retailing NVQs

F   Staff incompetence

G   The BHS response

H   Track record

I   Pay incentives and bonus schemes

J   Benefits for BHS and staff

K   Trail-blazers and market leaders

L   New decade – new approach

Example	*Answer*
Section I	L

1   Section II

2   Section III

3   Section IV

4   Section V

5   Section VI

Reading passage

NVQs in retailing – the BHS experience

Section I

In 1990, BHS, one of the UK's leading clothing retailers, made the radical decision to restructure the company and introduce new training and personnel policies which were linked to National Vocational Qualifications (NVQs) in retailing. The retailing NVQs have now become a central part of BHS's long-term commercial strategy for recovery and success. This initiative was launched under its 'First Choice' programme, which was designed to achieve a dramatic improvement in the performance of front-line staff. The strategy was to focus on and be driven by the customer, and to provide exceptional service. NVQs were to be the means by which BHS was to achieve this objective. BHS was breaking new ground not only within the company itself but also in the retail sector at large. BHS, alongside Boots and W H Smith, have now become trail-blazers and market leaders in the implementation of NVQs

Section II

In 1986 BHS became part of the Storehouse Group alongside Habitat and Mothercare. However, commercial success proved elusive. Whilst the retailing sector generally prospered, BHS did not. Staff performance was poor. Staff morale was low and attitudes towards management were negative. Staff turnover was far too high. Shop-floor staff were poorly rewarded and career prospects were very limited. Training was ineffective, focusing on knowledge and procedures, but not competence. It was divorced from line management. Shop-floor staff were trained independently from managers and there was little input by store managers into training policy. There were too many layers of management, making communication difficult. Shop-floor staff felt remote from management and were not involved in decision-making.

Section III

In 1989 a new management team was appointed with the brief to transform the company and put it on the road to success. New strategies were required for organizational change, customer service, and staff development and training. Layers of line management were stripped out of the organization. Store managers became fully responsible for recruitment and training. Shop assistants were to be called 'associates' to emphasize team work and partnership. Training was to become management driven within an integrated process of continuous staff development. The decision to introduce the retailing NVQs was taken from the top and was seen as being central to the company's wider human resource and organizational strategy. Furthermore, NVQs were to be the vehicle for the introduction of a performance-linked pay scheme, whilst providing a reliable measure of competence based on national standards.

Section IV

NVQs fitted in with BHS's philosophy of improving the performance, motivation and effectiveness of front-line staff. Pay incentives were offered on successful completion of the NVQs. This meant that BHS could now create a proper career structure to enable staff to progress within the organization, using the NVQ levels as staging posts. Staff would be trained and assessed on the job by in-store line managers and store managers would act as internal verifiers and countersigning officers.

Bonuses were offered to the stores in each region which achieved the best overall monthly figures. This system soon caught on, as the most successful stores tended to be those most effectively implementing the retailing NVQs.

City and Guilds was the chosen awarding body, supported by the National Retail Training Council (NRTC), which has been involved from the start in developing the standards underpinning the NVQs, in training assessors and verifiers, and in supporting promotional activities.

Section V

The scheme now feeds on its own success. Out of a workforce of 15,000, over 8,000 have been registered for NVQs since 1990. At present some 5,000 staff are registered for levels 1 and 2. Approximately 2,000 are qualified to level 1, and 500 to level 2. Many more will qualify soon, and level 3 is now on offer. Although BHS has recently moved towards a more flexible part-time system of working, replacing over 800 full-time jobs, staff who work more than 12 hours per week are automatically entered for the NVQ scheme. In fact, all new staff are required to work towards the NVQs, and eventually it is expected that all line and store managers will achieve NVQs at levels 3 and 4.

Section VI

Staff retention has increased dramatically. Staff morale, staff competence and commercial performance have improved significantly. BHS has bucked the trend[1] in this recession and increased its sales in 1992/3. The new career structure, underpinned by the retailing NVQs has enabled more women to become store managers, reversing the pattern before 1990. BHS's huge investment in NVQs, staff development and customer service has paid substantial dividends for the company. However, Kevin Heald, BHS Human Resource Director, says that 'the most significant and important factor for BHS staff is not just the additional remuneration they gain through NVQs, but the recognition they gain as individuals in achieving a qualification which is based on nationally recognized and approved standards. There is a sense of pride in this achievement which is reflected in the high levels of staff morale and motivation now present in the company. There is a pay-off for both company and staff'. Commitment from the top to NVQs is total, making BHS the biggest single participant in the NVQ system in the retail industry. It is not only a market leader in retailing – it also leads the way in showing how NVQs should be implemented and can work to the benefit of both organizations and individuals alike.

[1] been unusual

Question 6

6 According to the information in the text, how would you describe the decision to restructure BHS?

A fundamental

B peripheral

C superficial

D vocational

Write the appropriate letter (A–D) in box 6 on your answer sheet.

Questions 7–12

For each of the phrases in questions 7–12 say how they reflect the information in the reading passage, by writing:

S if it applies to staff,

SFS if it applies to shop-floor staff,

T if it applies to trainers, or

N if it is not clear to whom it applies.

Write your answers in boxes 7–12 on your answer sheet.

Example	*Answer*
poor performance	S

7 limited prospects

8 high turnover

9 ineffective procedures

10 no consultation

11 negative attitudes

12 not competent

Questions 13–16

Read the following statements and say how they reflect the information in the reading passage, by writing:

T   if it is true according to the passage,

F   it is false according to the passage, and

NCG if the information is not clearly given in the passage.

Write your answers in boxes 13–16 on your answer sheet.

Example   *Answer*

A new management team was   F

temporarily appointed.

13 Countersigning officers are trained at City and Guilds.

14 New staff must register for NVQs.

15 More women were store managers before the restructuring.

16 Both the company and staff are paid for implementing NVQs.

Reading passage

You are advised to spend about 20 minutes on the questions based on the reading passage below.

Harmful publications

Lack of culture, or rather an excess of the wrong sort of culture, is often considered to be synonymous with disadvantage. Most commonly associated with low cultural standards are low levels of reading, and some thirteen per cent of all twenty-three-year-olds feel they have trouble with reading and writing. One way of compensating such disadvantaged young people is thought to be to provide them with the culture they lack: in particular, high quality reading material.

Comic tragedy?

Whereas forty to fifty per cent of young people aged sixteen to twenty rarely read a book, the majority of young people appear to read comics. In 1991 sales of Viz, a UK comic, exceeded one million copies per issue, making it the fourth best-selling periodical in Britain. The reading of comics, however, is not restricted to young people: by 1992 it was estimated that two out of three men aged eighteen to fifty-three read Viz. The number of imitators this comic has spawned, including Zit, Gas, Brain Damage and Swiz, indicates the extent of the influence it wields.

The reading of comics was traditionally regarded by the educational establishment with considerable suspicion. Whereas the received arts were always assumed to exert an improving or civilizing influence, comics were thought to 'rot children's brains', to lower educational standards and to threaten morality. They were, and are, assumed to be an inferior cultural form, their readers assumed to come from the lower social classes, to be low educational attainers and to be easily led astray.

Over the past decade, perceptions of comics have shifted. Since the 1970s, the comic format has been commonly used to represent the interests of various disenfranchised groups – community groups, the unemployed, welfare recipients – who became more conscious of a climate conditioned by other contemporary movements such as civil rights, consumerism, self-help and de-institutionalization. As cultural signifiers, comics have become the subject matter of academic courses in cultural and media studies. Indeed, young people's cultural activities, grounded in the commercial rather than the subsidized sector, are beginning to merit the attention of the arts establishment.

Since the mid-1980s the comics market itself has boomed: the number of specialist shops and attendances at comics conventions has increased six-fold; the number of publishers and mainstream bookshops stocking comics has expanded; collecting comics was reported to be the fastest growing hobby, and, in the process, an adult readership has effectively 'come out'.

A survey carried out for Crisis, a fortnightly comic, clearly contradicted the stereo-typical image of a comics reader by revealing that two-thirds of its readers were aged sixteen to twenty-four, with the remaining third over twenty-five. Furthermore, the comic's readers were highly educated: over half were studying full- or part-time; nearly three-quarters read a quality daily. The comic's most popular stories focused on serious issues to do with the Third World and Northern Ireland.

Comics as education

The tone of educational comics has also changed. Twenty years ago it would have been considered immoral to produce advisory comics for prisoners, offering health advice for potentially illegal practices, not least because they would have appeared to condone the practices described. Yet comics are now considered to be the most effective medium for such advice, not least because they secure the interest of their target readership.

Certain British educationists, such as Margaret Meek, now advocate comics as educationally beneficial. This is because they encourage children and young people to read and contribute positively to the development of their fantasy play and to their acquisition of confidence and assurance. Yet, 150 years since they were first published, comics remain subject to the old prejudices, which maintain a particularly firm hold in schools.

Research is currently under way, in part prompted by curiosity as to why comics are still regarded with such disdain by the teaching profession. It is suspected that when comics are used in the classroom they are primarily given to children with learning difficulties, those learning English as a second language and those with behavioural problems; conversely, they are not given to children who have achieved higher educational standards. The research aims to establish to what extent comics are used in statutory and non-statutory education, what they are used for and what their potential might be. The resulting report focuses on the use of comics for and by disenfranchised young people, particularly those who may be denied access to the whole statutory curriculum and whose special educational needs are not adequately met.

Questions 17–21

The paragraph below is a summary of the first half of the reading passage. Complete the summary by selecting *three words* from the reading passage to complete the spaces numbered 17–21. Write the words in boxes 17–21 on your answer sheet.

The first one has been done for you as an example.

Summary: Harmful publications

Example   *Answer*

Low cultural standards are

often associated with dis-

advantage, such as low …   levels of reading

which is a difficulty experienced by many young adults. While around half of sixteen
to twenty-three year olds only rarely read books, most read comics. One of the … **17** …
in Britain is a comic, with a wide adult readership, and yet … **18** … still considers them
to be an … **19** …, appealing only to the lower levels of society. Attitudes are beginning
to change as … **20** … have adopted the format to present their views. The study of
certain aspects of comics even provides the content … **21** …, while the arts
establishment is also turning its attention to youth culture.

Questions 22–27

22 How many examples of an increase in sales of comics are given in the section on
Comics as education?

A   3

B   4

C   5

D   6

Write the appropriate letter (A–D) in box 22 on your answer sheet.

23 A survey of readers conducted for one of the publications showed that:

A   all readers of comics are at least 16 years old

B   most readers in the survey were highly educated

C   most readers of comics also read quality newspapers

D   readers of the most popular comics also read quality newspapers

Write the appropriate letter (A–D) in box 23 on your answer sheet.

24 According to the reading passage, comics have been proved to be the most effective
way of giving advice to prisoners.

Write:

A   if you agree with the statement above, or

D   if you disagree

in box 24 on your answer sheet.

25 According to the passage, schools agree with some educationists that comics are
educationally beneficial.

Write:

A   if you agree with the statement above, or

D   if you disagree with the statement above

in box 25 on your answer sheet.

26 Research is being conducted into aspects of the current use of comics in education. What other aspect does the research aim to establish?

Write *two words* in box 26 on your answer sheet.

27 Broadly speaking, do you think the authors feel that comics have educational value or that they should continue to be regarded with disdain?

Write either *have value* or *disdain* in box 27 on your answer sheet.

Reading passage

You are advised to spent about 20 minutes on the questions based on the reading passage below.

The urban revolution

The earth is witnessing an urban revolution, as people worldwide crowd into towns and cities. In 1800 only five per cent of the world's population were urban dwellers; now the proportion has risen to more than forty-five per cent, and by the year 2010 more people will live in towns and cities than in the countryside. Humanity will, for the first time, have become a predominantly urban species.

Though the world is getting more crowded by the day, absolute numbers of population are less important than where people concentrate and whether these areas can cope with them. Even densities, however, tell us nothing about the quality of the infrastructure – roads, housing and job creation, for example – or the availability of crucial services.

The main question, then, is not how many people there are in a given area, but how well their needs can be met. Density figures have to be set beside measurements of wealth and employment, the quality of housing and the availability of education, medical care, clean water, sanitation and other vital services. The urban revolution is taking place mainly in the Third World, where it is hardest to accommodate.

The move to towns

Between 1950 and 1985 the number of city dwellers grew more than twice as fast in the Third World as in industrialized countries. During this period, the urban population of the developed world increased from 477 million to 838 million, less than double; but it quadrupled in developing countries, from 286 million to 1.14 billion. Africa's urban population is racing along at five per cent a year on average, doubling city numbers every fourteen years. By the turn of the century, three in every four Latin Americans will live in urban areas, as will two in every five Asians and one in every three Africans. Developing countries will have to increase their urban facilities by two thirds by then, if they are to maintain even their present inadequate levels of services and housing.

The urban challenge

In 1940 only one out of every hundred of the world's people lived in a really big city, one with a population of over a million. By 1980 this proportion had already risen to one in ten. Two of the world's biggest cities, Mexico and São Paulo, are already bursting at the seams – and their populations are doubling in less than twenty years.

About a third of the people of the Third World's cities now live in desperately overcrowded slums and squatter settlements. Many are unemployed, uneducated, undernourished and chronically sick. Tens of millions of new people arrive every year, flocking in from the countryside in what is the greatest mass migration in history.

Pushed out of the countryside by rural poverty and drawn to the cities in the hope of a better life, they find no houses waiting for them, no water supplies, no sewerage, no schools. They throw up makeshift hovels, built of whatever they can find: sticks, fronds, cardboard, tar-paper, straw, petrol tins and, if they are lucky, corrugated iron. They have to take the land no-one else wants; land that is too wet, too dry, too steep or too polluted for normal habitation.

Yet all over the world the inhabitants of these apparently hopeless slums show extraordinary enterprise in improving their lives. While many settlements remain stuck in apathy, many others are gradually improved through the vigour and co-operation of their people, who turn flimsy shacks into solid buildings, build schools, lay out streets and put in electricity and water supplies.

Governments can help by giving the squatters the right to the land that they have usually occupied illegally, giving them the incentive to improve their homes and neighbourhoods. The most important way to ameliorate the effects of the Third World's exploding cities, however, is to slow down migration. This involves correcting the bias most governments show towards cities and towns and against the countryside. With few sources of hard currency, though, many governments in developing countries continue to concentrate their limited development efforts in cities and towns, rather than rural areas, where many of the most destitute live. As a result, food production falls as the countryside slides ever deeper into depression.

The demanding city

Since the process of urbanization concentrates people, the demand for basic necessities, like food, energy, drinking water and shelter, is also increased, which can exact a heavy toll on the surrounding countryside. High-quality agricultural land is shrinking in many regions, taken out of production because of over-use and mismanagement. Creeping urbanization could aggravate this situation, further constricting economic development.

The most effective way of tackling poverty, and of stemming urbanization, is to reverse national priorities in many countries, concentrating more resources in rural areas where most poor people still live. This would boost food production and help to build national economies more securely.

Ultimately, though, the choice of priorities comes down to a question of power. The people of the countryside are powerless beside those of the towns; the destitute of the countryside may starve in their scattered millions, whereas the poor concentrated in urban slums pose a constant threat of disorder. In all but a few developing countries the bias towards the cities will therefore continue, as will the migrations that are swelling their numbers beyond control.

Question 28

28 What do you think is the purpose of the reading passage?

A   to warn about the dangers of revolutions in towns

B   to warn about the possibility of a population explosion

C   to suggest governments should change their priorities

D   to suggest governments invest in more housing in cities

Write the appropriate letter (A–D) in box 28 on your answer sheet.

Questions 29–34

In each of questions 29–34 below, choose which of the answers best completes the sentence according to the information in the reading passage. For each question, write the appropriate letter (A–D) in boxes 29–34 on your answer sheet.

29 The urban population of the world …

A   has risen to around forty per cent in the last 200 years

B   will have risen to more than fifty per cent by the year 2010

C   has risen by forty-five per cent since 1800

D   will live in cities for the first time.

30 The most important factor is …

A   the quality of the infrastructure and services

B   where people are concentrated

C   wealth and employment

D   density figures and measurements.

31 The fastest growth in the rate of urbanization is in …

A   Africa

B   developing countries

C   Latin America

D   Asia

2 A third of the people in Third World cities …

A   live in Mexico and São Paulo

B   are undernourished and ill

C   live in inadequate housing

D   arrived last year

33 Many Third World city dwellers …

A   start their own business enterprises

B   create their own infrastructure and services

C   sleep in the streets

D   form people's co-operatives

34 Governments …

A   give incentives to improve the slums

B   give land to squatters

C   give preference to urban areas

D   give hard currency to cities and towns.

Questions 35–40

Complete the following summary by writing *up to three words* mainly from the text to complete spaces 35–40. Write the words in boxes 35–40 of your answer sheet.

The first one has been done for you an an example.

Summary: The urban revolution

Example   *Answer*

Increasing numbers of people have

migrated from the countryside

and moved into towns and cities

over the ...   last two centuries.

Most are in the Third World, where they are ... **35** ... accommodate because facilities
are at their most inadequate and meagre resources are most stretched. Many are
compelled to live in ... **36** ... with little chance of any ... **37** ... Furthermore, the process
of urbanization itself aggravates the situation by ... **38** ... Most governments nonetheless ... **39** ... spend their limited funds on urban problems, rather than putting their
efforts into rural areas where most of the poorest still live. The migration from the
countryside therefore seems ... **40** ...

Writing task 1

You should spend no more than 20 minutes on this task.

Study the following bar chart, which shows the expected growth in the population of some major cities by the year 2000.

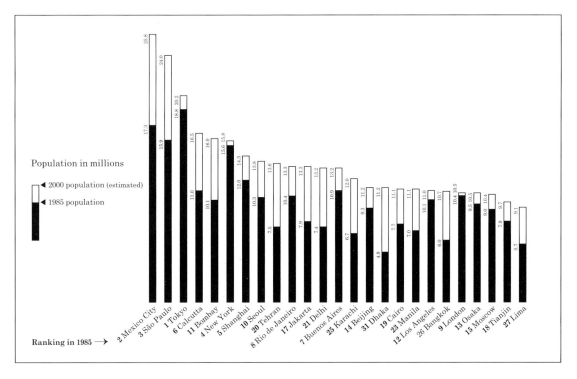

Figure 8 The world's twenty-five largest cities in the year 2000

Task:

Describe the most significant changes and pattern of change expected over the period.

You should write at least 150 words.

Writing task 2

You should spend no more than 40 minutes on this task.

There is a continuing migration from the countryside to urban areas in most countries of the world.

Task:

Write an essay for an educated reader on the following topic, stating to what extent you agree or disagree:

It is more important for governments to ensure adequate standards of housing, education and health care for their citizens by developing the industrial base than to use their resources to develop the rural areas.

You should write at least 250 words.

You should use your own ideas and experience and support your argument with examples.

Paper 4

Reading passage

You are advised to spend about 20 minutes on the questions based on the reading passage below.

Industrialization and development

During the 1980s development stagnated, and often regressed, in much of the Third World. A third of the entire population of the world lives in countries which experienced either zero growth or actual decline in the decade. More than forty Third World countries left the 1980s with lower per capita incomes than when they entered them and most fell even lower in 1990 and 1991.

The prices of the raw materials which poor countries sell to survive fell to record low levels, while the cost of manufactured goods that they import continued to rise. They became shackled with ever-increasing debts, paying about a quarter of their earnings to service them. Aid stagnated and bank lending to developing nations fell by almost two-thirds.

With falling commodity prices and the rising cost of manufactured goods, and an inability to industrialize, most developing countries are unable to pay off what they owe. Even increasing their commodity exports does not necessarily help. Sudan tripled its cotton exports between 1981 and 1983 but its revenue increased only marginally due to falling prices. Indeed, raising production helps to drive prices down. It can also do grave environmental damage by using the best land to grow cash crops and by increasing indiscriminate logging of tropical rainforests.

Third World exports

The economic pattern developed in the nineteenth century is still in operation: Third World countries overwhelmingly produce raw materials for export to richer countries. Third World economies depend on commodity prices: more than half rely on just one or two crops or minerals for over half of their foreign exchange. As the 1980s began, for example, Sudan's export earnings were sixty-five per cent dependent on cotton, Mauritius's sixty-eight per cent on sugar and Burundi's ninety-three per cent dependent on coffee. By 1987, the prices of thirty-three commodities monitored by the World Bank (excluding oil) stood at about half the 1960 level, falling by about forty per cent in the 1980s alone.

Falling demand: falling prices

Prices, largely determined by demand in the industrial world, have been kept low since the mid-1970s by recession and slow growth. Most agricultural commodities are produced by dozens of developing countries – sixty-two grow coffee – who compete for this same sluggish demand. If prices rise, rich countries can cut consumption, as many of the commodities, like bananas and coffee, are luxury items. Many more are being replaced by substitutes developed in wealthy countries: optical fibres are replacing copper wire in telecommunications, causing havoc for Zaire and Zimbabwe, while sugar substitutes in soft drinks have cut demand for sugar cane by around a quarter. These trends will continue, advances in biotechnology bringing a whole range of new substitutes, and there is little chance of prices recovering in the foreseeable future.

Industrialization

The Third World accounts for only 14.2 per cent of the world's industry and 60 per cent of this is in just nine countries, mainly in Asia and Latin America; least developed countries share just 0.21 per cent of world industry between them. If more developing countries industrialized they could earn more from their commodities by processing them and turning them into finished products, cutting their import bills at the same time. Unfortunately they face formidable obstacles. Most countries lack large home markets and have to sell as much as possible to the industrialized world – and indeed need to earn scarce foreign exchange. Even if there were a free market for their goods, however, it would not be easy to penetrate. Whilst they have the advantage of cheap labour and locally available raw materials, they have to face well-established rivals with markets and connections already set up, the best technology and science to hand, long production runs and mass production techniques.

Tariffs and barriers

Poor exporters generally have to overcome a series of tariffs and other barriers before they reach the well-protected markets of the technologically advanced rich. Generally speaking, semi-manufactured goods face tariffs which are double those for raw materials and finished goods are penalized twice as highly again. Non-tariff barriers, such as quotas, are even stricter. Together they are biased against developing countries: cloth imported into the European Community from poor countries faces tariffs four times as high as those imposed on other rich nations. The World Bank estimates that such trade barriers cost Third World countries between $50 and $100 billion a year.

Vulnerable industries are often concentrated in politically sensitive areas. Rather than embark on diversification and retraining programmes, governments find it easier to increase protection. Despite several international agreements designed to make access easier for Third World products, twenty of the world's twenty-four industrialized countries were more protectionist in 1992 than a decade before.

Stagnant aid

The United Nations Development Programme estimated in 1992 that the bias of the world's economy against developing countries costs them $500 billion a year, nearly ten times the amount they receive in aid. The UN target of 0.7% of GNP[1] in aid from richer countries is exceeded only by Norway, the Netherlands, Denmark and Sweden; the UK, Switzerland and the USA are among those that do not meet half this figure.

[1] Gross national product: the total annual income of a country

Questions 1–5

The reading passage gives several examples of changes which affected Third World development during the 1980s. Complete the table by selecting one item from the list of items (A–L) which affect development to fill each of the boxes (1–5), showing where there was an increase, no change or decrease.

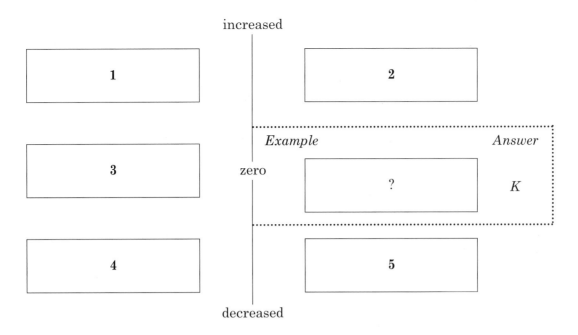

Write the appropriate letter (A–L) in boxes 1–5 on your answer sheet.

List of items

A   manufacturing

B   price of manufactured goods

C   per capita income

D   raw material production

E   import/export

F   aid

G   industrialization

H   price of commodities

I   debt

J   the best land

K   growth

L   bank lending

Questions 6–15

The paragraph below is a summary of the reading passage. Complete the summary by choosing *three words only* from the reading passage to fill the spaces numbered 6–15. Write the words in boxes 6–15 on your answer sheet.

The first one has been done for you as an example.

Summary: Industrialization and development

Example   *Answer*

A third of the world lives in

countries which experienced …   zero growth or

decline in the 1980s.

Whilst the cost of … **6** … debts rose, … **7** … bank lending, raw material prices and per capita incomes all fell. Unable to industrialize, Third World countries have become trapped by their dependence on only … **8** … commodities to earn much of their … **9** … Affected by … **10** … growth in the industrialized world, prices fell by almost half during the decade and are likely to remain low as a … **11** … synthetic substitutes further reduce demand. Ideally, developing countries … **12** … by processing their own commodities, simultaneously cutting the cost of imports. Unfortunately, they have very small … **13** … need the foreign exchange. It is not a free market internationally, however, as Third World countries lack their own trading connections and only have access to outdated technology and techniques. They are further penalized by restrictive … **14** … barriers, estimated to have cost them up to $100 billion a year. Despite agreements to encourage … **15** …, protectionism in industrialized nations actually increased over the period.

Reading passage

You are advised to spend about 20 minutes on the questions based on the reading passage below.

Handling the high flyers

A senior director describes his responsibilities in the Industrial Society's study Leaders: The learning curve of achievement: 'I am paid primarily to think, secondly to lead and direct, and lastly, to manage'. This could serve as a description of what is expected of senior managers. So how can the up-and-coming prepare themselves for this role? Here we look at how senior managers can be prepared for their responsibilities through training. The ingredients needed for successful senior management can be divided, for the sake of argument, into intellectual knowledge and personal qualities.

On the first count, let us assume that our aspiring manager is thoroughly numerate and possessed of a reasonable grasp of economic affairs, since this remains a fundamental basis for any senior managerial role. We will also assume that he or she has received, and absorbed, a fair amount of management training already, in such matters as time management, marketing, team building and people management – a fairly reasonable expectation today when the trend towards management education is gathering force in the UK. Finally, let us assume that the aspiring manager also has a sound technical knowledge, which is certainly not a far-fetched proposition, since promotion to senior management on the board often follows a strong performance in a specialist area. Moreover, while some skills, such as marketing, people management and finance are readily transferable, investment decisions in many cases would, presumably, demand a genuine technical understanding from those on the board. Often, too, senior managers need an understanding of technicalities to win the respect of professionals and technical staff – indeed, to communicate with them at a serious level.

It is the ability to move from being a specialist to a generalist that is all important for a manager wanting to assume a more senior role. Patricia Marshall of Hay/McBer management consultancy calls this transition the 'paradigm shift'. One problem that recurs, says Andrew Forrest of the Industrial Society is that people join the board with experience of only one function, such as finance or marketing, when what is needed, intellectually speaking, is vision, maturity, and the ability to think laterally and logically beyond specialist confines.

Just as important is the need to think internationally – if not globally, then certainly in European terms. In addition, senior managers need to have a firm grasp of strategy in order to make fundamental long-term choices which will shape the course of a business – such as the choice of markets or whether or not to demerge a business.

This broader, more self-critical and strategic outlook can be cultivated in a number of ways. Forrest believes it is vital that managers assuming director-level responsibilities get outside their own organization – go abroad, go to business school, talk to the City, the media, customers – so that they learn to see their company from the outside.

Non-executive directorships can be a route to directorial enlightenment. One of the best ways of learning to be a good executive director is to be the non-executive director of another company. Directors have to stand back and view themselves and where they are taking their business, which is enormously difficult because people, on the whole, are not self-critical and tend to become defensive. As a non-executive director of another company, one can see in others what one's own colleagues will be looking for in oneself. As a result, quite a number of company chairman now instruct their executive directors to take on non-executive directorships; everyone benefits from the experience.

The business schools, of course, provide a variety of short management courses aimed at improving managers' perception. One particularly effective one is the intensive three-week senior manager programme (SMP) at Cranfield School of Management. It has been specifically devised to get its students to think and act as 'strategists, leaders, and global managers'. Some 100 high-flying managers from around the world attend the course every year. Programme director and lecturer David Butcher says that the priorities of the course are in line with the best management thinking and theory of today. The current emphasis on leadership, for example, corresponds with the need for greater individual contributions from all levels of today's corporations. This is due to the fashion for less hierarchical structures.

Cranfield, like most business schools runs both public programmes (such as the SMP) and courses tailored to specific companies. Each has its advantages. Managers attending the latter will be working towards the same goals, so they will explore business issues in greater depth, and people can also be developed in relationship with each other. On the other hand, the advantage of the public SMP, says Butcher, is the scope for individual attention and development (this would be less practical for managers working within the same company). It also gives trainees insights into other organizations and the opportunity to build up an international network.

Most forward-thinking companies groom their brightest and best senior management through a blend of management training courses, both public and tailor-made, and carefully-plotted job appointments and secondments. Indeed, provided the company is sufficiently international in scope and diverse in character, secondments abroad are invaluable.

The Industrial Society offers smaller organizations short (one-week) attachments within organizations. Outside managers are seconded to other companies that can help them solve a real problem. For instance, a civil servant was sent to the Chester Chronicle and was able to design a newspaper on youth employment when he returned to work. The Industrial Society has arranged over 1,400 such attachments. Forrest believes this is an excellent way of learning.

So far, it is mainly the intellectual aspects of management development that have been explored. But the 'paradigm shift' necessary for a manager to become a director also involves developing personal skills and ways of handling people. Marshall at Hay/McBer claims that the move from functional head to director status involves thinking about how best to co-operate with one's peers, rather than simply directing subordinates, and influencing other people without giving direct orders.

At the GHN consultancy, which specializes in mentoring (the training term for coaching) for senior managers, corporate relations director Susan Bloch says that the modern manager needs to learn to balance skills, acting at times as project manager, at times as team member. There are some situations which require authoritative behaviour, others which need a more consultative approach. She stresses that communication at all levels (from the way you talk to the way you dress) is all-important. She also believes that high flyers need to think about politics and internal networking.

Personal coaching (or mentoring) is an effective way of building up these – and other – personal skills. Indeed, Forrest at the Industrial Society recommends that all companies consider setting up a mentoring scheme, although he stresses that the art of mentoring is a subtle one. Sheila Forbes at Reed Elsevier sees a further role for it in the development of such qualities as the courage to take risks and the ability to cope with uncertainty.

Questions 16–19

List the *four* areas of competence which the author assumes will be possessed by a manager aspiring to senior manager status.

Write a maximum of *two words* for each answer in boxes 16–19 on your answer sheet.

Questions 20–21

Read the following statements and say how they reflect the information in the reading passage, by writing:

T   if it accurately reflects the information given;

F   if it does not reflect the information in the passage;

?   if the information is not clearly given in the passage.

Write your answers in boxes 20–21 on your answer sheet.

Example	*Answer*
According to one senior director, his intellectual abilities are more highly valued than his personal qualities.	T

20 Successful managers must broaden their range of abilities rather than developing their specialized skills.

21 Many companies now insist that managers take on a non-executive directorship before they can become executive directors.

Questions 22–26

In questions 22–26, choose which of the endings (A–J) in the list below best completes the sentence according to the information in the reading passage.

Write the appropriate letter in boxes 22–26 on your answer sheet.

List of endings

A   flatter company hierarchies

B   interpersonal relationships

C   international networks

D   international secondments

E   long-term, international thinking

F   tackle genuine problems

G   individual contributions

H   effective strategies

I   design newspapers

J   training and appropriate experience

22   One short management course aims to develop …

23   The course reflects the needs within today's …

24   Cranfield's private course allows for greater concentration on …

25   Most senior managers are selected and prepared for their positions by means of …

26   Secondments allow managers to experience other organizations and …

Questions 27–28

In the reading passage two different claims are made as being the key to success for management at director level. State these qualities by writing a *maximum of two words* for each answer in boxes 27–28 on your answer sheet.

Questions 29–30

29   From the information in the text, which of the following answers best describes 'mentoring'?

A   it is stressful

B   it is difficult to do well

C   it requires courage

D   it is most effective with the arts

Write the appropriate letter (A–D) in box 29 on your answer sheet.

30   How many benefits of mentoring are mentioned in the text?

Write a number in box 30 on your answer sheet.

Reading passage

You are advised to spend about 20 minutes on the questions based on the reading passage below.

Problems with contaminated land in the UK

'The polluter pays' principle.

Those with an interest in land which is contaminated with noxious substances, or has been put to a use which makes it liable to be so contaminated, are growing increasingly concerned that the land may carry with it liabilities for clean-up costs or compensation to third parties. The UK has followed the EC in endorsing the general principle that 'the polluter pays'. However, this principle extends not just to those who are primarily responsible for causing any contamination, and the resulting damage to the environment, but also to others who merely have an interest in the land in question.

Who is potentially liable?

Anyone causing or permitting pollution is clearly at risk, and this may involve both criminal and civil liability. In the case of criminal offences by a corporate body, certain individuals could be personally liable for offences for which they are responsible.

Where the 'owner' is made liable for clean-up costs, it is not clear precisely who is covered by this. In the Environmental Protection Act 1990, for example, there is no definition of 'owner' and it appears to have been the Government's intention that this should be the party with the most immediately relevant interest. However, if that party is not in a position to meet financial obligations, then one can expect that others may be the subject of claims. This may extend to mortgagees, especially where a lender enforces its security by taking possession of land, and possibly also in other circumstances where it exercises a degree of control. Lending institutions are currently looking anxiously in the direction of Brussels to see the extent to which lenders are going to be able to avoid being caught for liabilities greater than the value of their security.

The impact on land transactions

Buying and selling land

The principle of caveat emptor[1] *still applies in UK land transactions and the seller is not obliged to disclose the existence of contamination. However, the seller will be in a stronger position if he has good information as to the state of the premises. Thus a seller may carry out his own environmental audit of the site and will usually find it advantageous to disclose the resulting information to a prospective purchaser. In certain cases the seller may obtain an indemnity from the purchaser where premises are sold subject to declared defects or outstanding environmental problems. The purchaser for his part will be seeking the best possible information, preferably backed with warranties from the seller and, if possible, coupled with an indemnity from the seller.*

Lending

The lender's concerns are similar to those of the purchaser. Where there is the possibility of contamination, the preliminary investigations must be sufficient to enable a lender to make a reasonable assessment of risks. The loan documentation should include appropriate warranties, covenants and events of default. Care also needs to be taken in enforcing security so that action is not taken by the lender which could open the door to environmental liabilities.

Leasing

When granting a lease of land, and owner will need to be careful not only to avoid exposure to liability during the term of the lease but, even more, to prevent the situation arising whereby he inherits a liability on the termination of the lease. Thus, it would be prudent for the landlord to control more closely the use to which the premises are put, as well as including expressed covenants on the part of the tenant not to cause pollution.

[1] Latin phrase meaning 'let the buyer beware'

Questions 31–35

Read the following statements and indicate how they reflect the information in the reading passage, by writing:

T   if the statement is true,

F   if it is false, or

NC   if it is not clear from the passage.

Write your answers in boxes 31–35 on your answer sheet.

Example   *Answer*

Britain has persuaded the EC

to adopt the 'polluter pays'

principle.   F

31   Impending legislation on the pollution of land will probably only apply to land which has already been polluted.

32   Those holding an interest in contaminated land will be made liable for clean-up costs and compensation.

33   Responsibility extends to the owners of the property as well as those who cause any contamination.

34   Individuals within companies may be personally liable for criminal and civil offences committed on land owned by their company.

35   Owners who simply lend property to individuals and companies may also be made liable.

Questions 36–40

36   Both the seller and the purchaser want detailed information on the state of the property. How does the seller obtain this?

Write up to *three words* as your answer in box 36 on your answer sheet.

37–38 As well as information on the state of the property, what two other assurances will a purchaser seek?

Write *one word only* for each answer in boxes 37–38 on your answer sheet.

39   What extra precaution needs to be taken in lending rather than buying and selling?

Write *two words* as your answer in box 39 on your answer sheet.

40   At which point is it most important that owners who lease property make sure they are not being exposed to liability?

Write *no more than four words* as your answer in box 40 on your answer sheet.

Writing task 1

You should spend no more than 20 minutes on this task.

Study the graphs in figure 9 below, which show how much food is produced per head in different parts of the world.

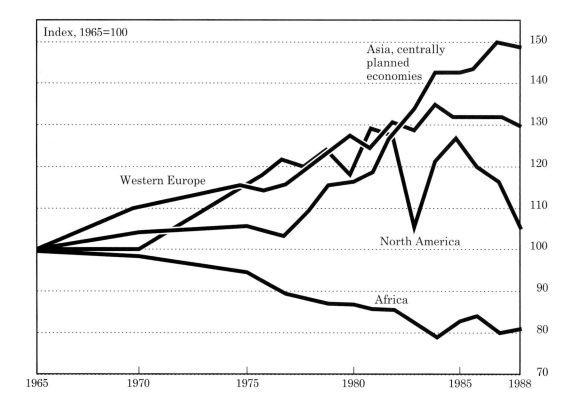

Figure 9 World per capita food production

Task:

Write a short essay, describing the information and trends shown in the graph.

You should write at least 150 words.

Writing task 2

You should spend no more than 40 minutes on this task.

Task:

Write an essay for a university lecturer on the following topic:

Business education and training today must promote environmental awareness.

You should write at least 250 words.

You should use your own ideas and experience and support your argument with examples.

Supplementary writing tests

Writing task 1

You should spend no more than 20 minutes on this task.

The reading passage on pp. 15–6 describes the socio-cultural impact of tourism. The table and figure below show tourist arrivals and departures in Cyprus between 1976 and 1989, and composition by length of stay.

Table 4 Composition of tourist departures by length of stay (%)

Time-band	1977	1983	1988
< 1 month	81.3	88.4	93.9
1 – 2 months	13.1	8.1	4.1
> 2 months	5.1	2.7	1.0
not stated	0.5	0.8	1.0

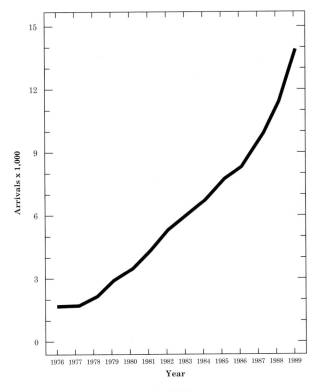

Figure 10 International tourist arrivals 1976-89

Task:

Describe the trends in tourist numbers and length of stay over the period.

You should write at least 150 words.

Writing task 2

You should spend no more than 40 minutes on this task.

Task:

Discuss the following:

Whilst studying abroad provides an opportunity to broaden one's experience, it also presents the danger of negative influences from the host culture.

You should write at least 250 words.

You should use your own ideas and experience and support your argument with examples.

Writing task 1

You should spend no more than 20 minutes on this task.

The reading passage on pp. 23–25 describes the importance of reading skills in tertiary education. Look at the figure below, which shows primary school enrolment and the adult literacy rate in some developing countries.

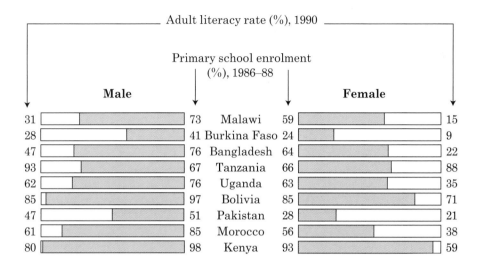

Figure 11 Literacy and school enrolment

Task:

Describe the pattern of adult literacy and school enrolment, and any relationship between the two.

You should write at least 150 words.

Writing task 2

You should spend no more than 40 minutes on this task.

Technological advances continue to improve manufacturing efficiency; the weight of a drinks can has come down from thirty-five grams to about fifteen grams, for example, and modern cars and production techniques are much more energy efficient.

Task:

Write an essay for a university lecturer on the following topic:

Governments need to control the environment rather than controlling industry, as companies already control their resources very efficiently.

You should write at least 250 words.

You should use your own ideas and experience and support your argument with examples.

Writing task 1

You should spend no more than 20 minutes on this task.

The pie charts below show the energy consumption and sources of energy for several areas of the world.

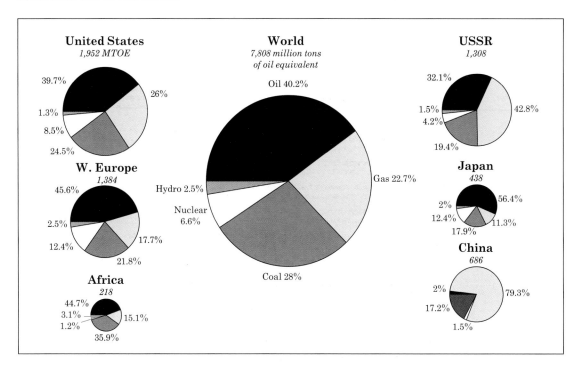

Figure 12 Energy consumption % breakdown, 1991

Task:

Describe the similarities and differences as shown in the charts.

You should write at least 150 words.

Writing task 2

You should spend no more than 40 minutes on this task.

Task:

Present a case to a funding agency arguing either for or against the following statement:

Training for work is far more important than providing a broad-based education.

You should write at least 250 words.

You should use your own ideas and experience and support your argument with examples.

Writing task 1

You should spend no more than 20 minutes on this task.

There is a steady, growing migration of people from the land to the city. Study the figure below, which shows the number of people living in squatter settlements in some major cities.

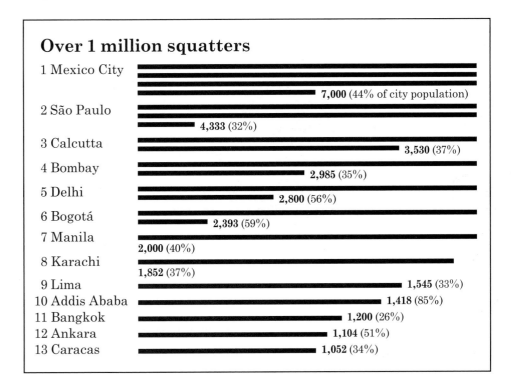

Figure 13   Informal (squatter) settlements
Number of people living in squatter settlements in
selected major cities, 1980s (figures in thousands)

Task:

Describe the information presented in the figure.

You should write at least 150 words.

Writing task 2

You should spend no more than 40 minutes on this task.

Task:

Write an essay for an academic adviser on the following question:

What steps should a student take in preparing for tertiary education and what would be the benefit of taking such steps?

You should write at least 250 words.

You should use your own knowledge and experience and support your argument with examples.

Writing task 1

You should spend no more than 20 minutes on this task.

Look at the figures for the proportion of people involved in agriculture, as shown in the pie charts below.

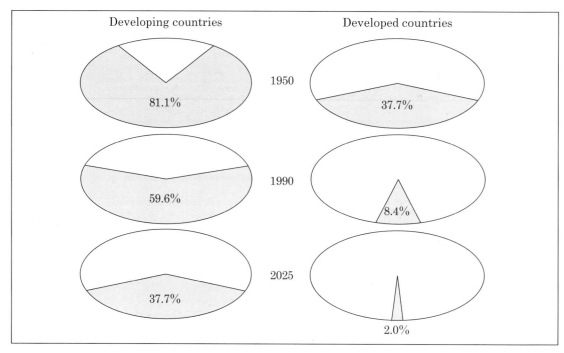

Figure 14 Percentage of population engaged in agriculture

Task:

Describe the information and trends shown.

You should write at least 150 words.

Writing task 2

You should spend no more than 40 minutes on this task.

Almost three-quarters of the population of the developed world live in towns and cities, whereas around two-thirds of the developing world live in rural areas.

Task:

Argue for or against the following statement:

The developed world should lead by example and not insist that aid to the Third World is used to develop rural areas.

You should write at least 250 words.

You should use your own ideas and experience and support your argument with examples.

Select bibliography

Any good grammar or course book should help you to improve your English. Most course books have accompanying cassettes for listening practice and some have tapes of drills for speaking practice. See what is available in your local bookshop or library.

For IELTS you can concentrate on the areas where you feel you need extra help. Study skills material may be particularly useful. The following titles will help your further study.

Reading

Glendinning, E. and **Holmston, B.** *Study reading*, Cambridge University Press, 1992

Haarman, L. *Reading skills for the social sciences*, Oxford University Press, 1988

Jordan, R. *Looking for information*, Longman, 1980

Morrow, K. *Skills for reading*, with extracts from *New Scientist*, Oxford University Press, 1980

Nolan Woods, E. and others *Penguin advanced reading skills*, Penguin, 1986

Thomas, B. *Practical information, comprehension and composition practice*, Edward Arnold, 1977

Writing

Fletcher, M. and **Hargreaves, R.** *Defining and verbalizing*, Evans Brothers, 1980

Glendinning, E. and **Mantell, H.** *Write ideas: an intermediate course in writing skills*, Longman, 1983

Hamp-Lyons, L. and **Beasley, B.** *Study writing*, Cambridge University Press, 1987

Johnson, K. *Communicate in writing*, Longman, 1981

Jolly, D. *Writing tasks*, Cambridge University Press, 1984 (especially chapters 6 and 7)

Listening

Blundell, L. and **Stokes, J.** *Task listening*, Cambridge University Press, 1981

Boyd, T. *In their own words*, Nelson, 1988

Jones, L. *Ideas: speaking and listening activities*, Cambridge University Press, 1984

Lynch, T. *Study listening: understanding lectures and talks in English*, Cambridge University Press, 1983

Maley, A. and **Moulding, S.** *Learning to listen*, Cambridge University Press, 1981

Scarborough, D. *Reasons for listening*, Cambridge University Press, 1984

Speaking

Baker, A. *Ship or sheep? An intermediate pronunciation course*, Cambridge University Press, 1977

Baker, A. *Tree or Three,* Cambridge University Press, 1982

Bradford, B. *Intonation in context*, Cambridge University Press, 1985

Collie, J. and **Slater S.** *Speaking 2*, Cambridge University Press, 1992

Doff, A. and **Jones, C.** *Feelings*, Cambridge University Press, 1980

Geddes, M. and **Sturtridge, G.** *Advanced conversation*, Macmillan, 1992

Jones, L. see **Listening**

Kench, A. B. *Asking questions*, Macmillan, 1970

Lynch, T. and **Anderson, K.** *Study speaking*, Cambridge University Press, 1992

Morgan, J. and **Rinvolucri, M.** *The Q book: practising interrogatives in reading, speaking and writing*, Longman, 1988

Mortimer, C. *Elements of pronunciation*, Cambridge University Press, 1985

Ramsey, G. and **Rees-Parnell, H.** *Well spoken*, Longman, 1989

Study skills

Adkins, A. and **McKean I.** *Text to note*, Nelson, 1983

Buzan, T. *Use your head*, BBC Books, 1974, 1982

Collins, *Study skills in English (series)*, Collins

Forman, D. and others *Campus English*, Macmillan, 1990

Heaton, J. *Studying in English*, Longman, 1975

McAlpin, J. *The Longman dictionary skills handbook*, Longman, 1989

Smith, J. and **Coffey, B.** *English for study purposes*, Macmillan, 1982 (Part 1 and Part 2)

Smith, M. and **Smith, G.** *A study skills handbook*, Oxford University Press, 1990

Underhill, A. *Use your dictionary*, Oxford University Press, 1980

Wallace, M. *Study skills in English*, Cambridge University Press, 1980

Waters, M. and **Waters, A.** *Study tasks in English*, Cambridge University Press, 1996

Wilberg, P. and **Lewis, M.** *Business English*, Language Teaching Publications, 1990

Dictionaries and grammars

Williams, R. *Panorama: advanced course of English for study and examinations*, Longman, 1982

Collins Cobuild English language dictionary, Collins, 1987

Longman active study dictionary of English, Longman, 1983

Oxford advanced learner's dictionary of current English, Oxford University Press, 1989 (4th ed.)

Allsop, J. *English grammar*, Cassell, 1983

Eastwood, J. *Oxford practice grammar,* Oxford University Press, 1992

Leech, G. and **Svartvik, J.** *A communicative grammar of English*, Longman, 1975

Murphy, R. *English grammar in use*, Cambridge University Press, 1985

Swan, M. *Practical English usage*, Oxford University Press, 1981

Tapescript

Section 1

Ana Maria is talking to her friend Abdul on the telephone. They are arranging to meet later and go into the college together. Look at the example and questions 1–4.

For each of the questions, decide which picture, A, B, C or D is the best answer and circle the letter in your book. First, listen to the example.

Ana Maria If you want to catch your train, you'd better go now. It must be nearly half past already.

Abdul Wow! you're right … and it goes just after half past. That's in less than ten minutes. I didn't realise it was so late. I'd better run – see you around twelve-thirty – 'bye.

Ana Maria 'bye.

Voice over Ana Maria says it's nearly half past. Adbul says the train goes just after half past, which is in less than ten minutes. The only possible answer is C. So you circle C.

Now you will hear the complete recording for section one. Answer the questions as you listen because you will hear the recording once only; First, have another look at questions 1–4.

Now you will hear the recording.

Listen carefully and circle the appropriate letter for each question.

Ana Maria It's not a bad journey, really.

Abdul But what do I do when I get there? How do I get to your place?

Ana Maria Don't worry – I'll meet you in town. When you get to Waterloo, take the underground to Regent's Park. You can turn either right or left from the exit, then take the first turning you come to. It doesn't matter which – it's a crescent – either way you'll come into Portland Place. It's a wide street – you can't miss it. Then take the second on the right – just keep going straight on as far as you can – that'll take you into the High Street. I'll meet you there – outside the pub on the corner. When are you leaving?

Abdul I'm ready now. I'll get the … the 1134, I think it is, that's non-stop to Waterloo. And I get the underground there?

Ana Maria That's it – hop straight on the tube there. You want the Bakerloo to Regent's Park – it's only about four stops. Make sure you get a northbound train though – you want northbound Bakerloo, OK?

Abdul OK – I'll be there soon.

Ana Maria Oh, by the way, I'll be with Tom – we're going to play badminton later, so we'll have all our sports gear. But look – if you want to catch your train, you'd better go now. It must be nearly half past already.

Abdul Wow! you're right … and it goes just after half past. That's in less than ten minutes. I didn't realise it was so late. I'd better run – see you around twelve-thirty – 'bye.

Ana Maria 'bye.

Voice over Now look at questions 5–10. Ana Maria and Tom have persuaded Abdul to join the college badminton club. He is talking to the club secretary. As you listen, fill in the spaces 5–10 on the membership form. First you have some time to look at the form.

Now listen carefully and fill in gaps 5–10

Secretary Well, if you could just give me some details – first, your name.

Abdul Abdul.

Secretary Is that your first name or family name?

Abdul First name – my family name is Amin.

Secretary Amin – how do you spell that?

Abdul A M I N

Secretary Right – which faculty?

Abdul Computer studies … electronics.

Secretary Electronics? So the faculty – that's engineering and science, is it?

Abdul Yes – sorry – I'm doing the electronics foundation course.

Secretary O. K. foundation. That must be F. So you're a fresher – have you joined the students' union?

Abdul Yes – do you want to see my card?

Secretary I just need your SU number – let's see – here we are – nine two Y G three oh double four. Where are you living?

Abdul I'm in the halls of residence – Spring Court.

Secretary Aah right – Spring Court – which number?

Abdul 36 … 36D.

Secretary Great – last two questions: How do you rate your game – beginner? – league?

Abdul Oh no – I'm not league standard – just middling really – not bad – but not good. I just play for fun and to keep fit.

Secretary Fine. And … how long've you been playing?

Abdul Oooh – three or four years, I suppose.

Secretary Great, well that's it – welcome to the club. When you want a game, you book a court over there. OK?

Abdul Great – thanks. 'bye

Voice over That is the end of section 1. You now have some time to check your answers.

Voice over That is the end of section 1. In the IELTS test you would now go on to section 2. For this exercise, though, you may check your answers for this section with the book before you go on. If you want to check your answers stop the tape now.

Now turn to section 2.

Section 2

You are going to hear a description of services which are provided by the college library. Three different speakers each describe one of the services. First, read questions 11–20.

Now listen to section 2 and do questions 11–20.

Voice one Welcome to Central College library services. We have a well-stocked bank of resources which are in three main locations: the library itself, with books and periodicals; the self-access language centre, with audio and video material; and the micro-computer lab. I'll start with the library as you have to pass through it in order to reach the other two. We have two main sections for books and another for periodicals and journals. The books are in two categories: general loan and reference. Up to four general loan books may be taken out for up to three weeks by full-time students. Loans may be renewed if no one has requested the title. Please note, however, that some of the most popular coursebooks are available on twenty-four-hour loan. The other category which includes our very extensive range of dictionaries is titles which are available for reference only; they may not be taken out of the library under any circumstances. All titles can be located using our Biblitas cataloguing system. There are three computer terminals linked to Biblitas or there is the micro-fiche system for those who find it easier. Both the Biblitas and micro-fiche catalogues list publications under author and title and both are very easy to use; the Biblitas system has the advantage of having a separate subject index. Now, for a description of the self-access learning centre, I'd like you to listen to the pre-recorded cassette on the machines over there.

Voice two The self-access language centre is across the corridor directly opposite the reference section of the library, next to the micro-lab. Go through the door at the far end of the library to reach both the centre and the lab. In the self-access centre we have both audio and video material and extensive playback facilities. There are ten audio and six video playback machines. We also have four mini audiolabs, where you can record your own responses to exercises on the tapes. As well as audio and video players, there are three computer terminals for CALL materials; that is computer aided language learning: C A double L 'CALL' for short. All the playback machines, with the exception of computer monitors, are fitted with headphones, so as not to disturb other users. This applies also to the two television receivers, which are tuned in to receive satellite broadcasts in French, German, Italian, Spanish and Russian. There are six headphone sockets and headsets with each satellite television receiver, but they are very popular at news times. Times of news broadcasts from each of the five countries are given on the desk between the televisions. There is always someone in the centre for advice on both technical matters and on choosing the most suitable materials for your study. You may, of course, bring your own materials to the language learning centre, but no materials may be taken away – they must all be used and retained in the centre. Finally, the centre is open during normal library hours, that is from nine till seven on weekdays and from eleven to three on Saturday and Sunday.

Voice three Right, everybody – my name's Kathy Jenkins – I'll take you through to the micro-lab and tell you a little about that before we leave you to explore for yourselves. So – here we are – come on – right through to the middle. Now the micro-computing lab, or micro-lab as we call it, is fitted with twenty-seven stand-alone terminals; twenty-four PCs and three Macs. If you are a member of the library, you may borrow CALL disks in any of five foreign languages as well as English. You may also borrow a range of wordprocessing and desktop publishing packages. All disks are, of course, strictly for use in the micro-lab only. If you wish to print anything you should use one of the six machines around the outside of the room. Four are connected to dot-matrix printers, one is connected to the laser printer and the sixth is connected to the plotter. If you want a top quality printout from the laser printer or the plotter, come and see myself or any of the library staff. Dot-matrix printouts are free but there is a charge for using the other printers. There is always a queue to get to the terminals towards the end of term. Come in and get to know how to use the terminals early in the term and use them regularly, rather than just before exams and essay deadlines, in order to avoid delay or disappointment. Training sessions are held on a regular basis, on the first and third Thursday of each month, and are free to full-time students of the college. See you there. Now, any questions?

Voice over That is the end of section 2. You now have a minute to check your answers to questions 11–20.

Voice over That is the end of section 2. In the IELTS test you would now go on to section 3. For this exercise, though, you may check your answers for this section with the book before you go on. If you want to check your answers stop the tape now.

Now turn to section 3.

Section 3

Later, Ana Maria goes to talk to her personal tutor. You will hear an extract from their discussion. As you listen, answer questions 21–29. First you have some time to look at questions 21–29. Now, listen carefully to the conversation between Ana Maria and her tutor and answer questions 21–29.

Tutor Have you settled in?

Ana Maria Yes, I feel quite at home now. I haven't got used to the food yet but I'm enjoying the life on campus.

Tutor Good. Now we'd better make sure you enjoy your studies. We offer a very wide range of options on the foundation course, as you know; but you can only take six modules – do you know what you want to do yet?

Ana Maria Yes, more or less, but I'm not sure whether to do biological sciences or German.

Tutor Well, that's quite a difference. You want to do computer studies, don't you?

Ana Maria Mmmmm, yeh.

Tutor Well, let's see – you elected to do: physical sciences, basic electronics, art and design C.A.D. – that computers and design – isn't it?

Ana Maria Computer-aided design actually, 'CAD', but …

Tutor Oh, right – anyway, CAD and … and English. That's quite a range. Don't you want to do maths – or computer programming, for example? Why d'you choose to do art and design?

Ana Maria Well, I'm interested in electronics – in computers – especially in writing computer games. I'd like to produce educational software, educational games, eventually. I've taught myself a lot of programming – I … I don't think I'd benefit much from a foundation level course.

Tutor No … no, I see that – go on.

Ana Maria So, er, I want the basics – the physical science and electronics – I was hopeless at physics at school and we didn't have electronics – but I was good at maths – I don't think I need that.

Tutor … and the art and design?

Ana Maria That will be good for my graphics – I need that to produce games – CAD too – I've never done CAD before.

Tutor No – right – they've got some powerful packages in the computer graphics and CAD offices – you'll enjoy that. So … that leaves English. It's mostly English lit. I know your English is very good, but did you know you can take English as a foreign language as one of the modules in the foundation year?

Ana Maria No … no, I didn't. That's great – if they've got classes at my level. I don't have any problem speaking – but my writing is terrible.

Tutor Oh, I'm sure they have – go and talk to them in the EAP department – oh, and I suggest you join the study skills classes, too. They'll have sessions on report writing and so on.

Ana Maria Great – I really need some help with my writing, especially spelling.

Tutor Well that would be in the EFL classes – study skills would help more with how to structure your essays and so on … now, your last module …

Ana Maria Yeh … well … I gave up biology at school to do physics – but I much prefer biology – I'd like to study some more while I can but German is very important in technical subjects, so I want to do that too.

Tutor Well, you could do it as an option next year – you do know that?

Ana Maria No, I didn't – I mean, I didn't check.

Tutor Yes … yes, I think that's the thing to do – concentrate on your English this year – you could take Cambridge proficiency – and you'll need IELTS for the first year of the degree – start the German next year.

Ana Maria Right – that sounds good.

Tutor Good – well, if you have any problems academic or otherwise, just come and see me.

Ana Maria OK – thanks.

Tutor I'm on extension 7459.

Ana Maria 7459.

Tutor That's it – just leave a message if I'm not in the office – OK, if there's nothing else …

Ana Maria No … no, that's fine, thanks.

Tutor Good-bye for now then.

Ana Maria 'bye.

Voice over That is the end of section 3. You now have half a minute to check your answers.

Voice over That is the end of section 3. In the IELTS test you would now go on to section 4. For this exercise, though, you may check your answers for this section with the book before you go on. If you want to check your answers stop the tape now.

Now turn to section 4.

Section 4

You will now hear a recording of part of Ana Maria's first lecture on study skills. First you will have some time to look at Ana Maria's notes, and the gaps 31–35, as well as questions 36–38.

As you listen to the lecture fill in the gaps numbered 31–35. Answer questions 36–38 by writing a T if the information is true, an F is the information is false or a question mark if the information is not given. Now you will hear the lecture.

Lecturer Well, I'd like to begin by saying how pleased I am that so many of you have come to the first of our study skills sessions this term. In the past, many students have said how much they have appreciated the classes. 'Why didn't they tell me that at school?' is one of the most frequent remarks. Further education is quite different from being at school, as I am sure you're finding out. You will be treated more as an equal – but you will also be expected to be much more independent. This means that there is far more pressure on you to take your own decisions – such as working out a study programme – and sticking to it. I'll give you our programme for the term during the break, by the way. You may also find that you are asked to do things in a different way from classes at school – taking part in seminars and tutorials, for example. That is going to be the theme of this evening: speaking skills. I'll refer to writing from time to time because I am not going to talk about pronunciation – I am talking more about the ways in which we structure discourse in English, the way we organize what we say. All too soon you will need to do this – when you are asked to present your ideas on a particular topic – in a seminar – or in writing – or both. I think it would be as well to run through some of the conventions that we generally use. Much of this may be familiar to some of you but I think it is worth saying again. I shall cover three areas: first, the beginning … a good introduction; then, the middle … making your point effectively, giving examples and linking it all together logically; and finally, the end … coming to a good conclusion. Today we'll also look at ways of agreeing – and disagreeing – even ways of interrupting and taking the floor – but first I'd like each of you to take a clean sheet of paper – now divide the page vertically into three columns – about the same size if you can – head the one on the left 'function' – the other two are one for speaking and one for writing – now the column on the left …

Voice over That is the end of section 4. You now have half a minute to check your answers.

That is almost the end of the test. You now have one more minute to check all your answers.

That is the end of the test. Stop writing now.

Answer key

Section one: practice

Reading

Exercise 1

1 We know it is about a beetle; its life cycle; 'hidden' implies that the life cycle occurs inside something; 'history' may refer to the life cycle or to the development of the species over time.

2 paragraph 3

3 paragraph 2

4 paragraph 1

Exercise 2

5 oak

6 willow

7 by fungi

8 stored reserves

9 ten (10) years

10 late summer/early autumn

Exercise 3

11 F

12 B

13 E

14 B C D E

15 somatic sensory cortex.

Exercise 4

16 NCG

17 NCG

18 F

19 A

20 D

21 F

Exercise 5

22 C

23 F

24 liberalization of world markets

25 sophisticated communications systems

26 three/3

Exercise 6

27 high frequency

28 roll slowly

29 –

30 normal/deep sleep

31 large/slow waves

32 still

33 –

34 jerk rapidly

35 paralysed

36 B

37 A

Exercise 7

38 TD

39 D

40 T

41 T

42 TD

43 T

44 TD

45 three/3

46 quicker; simpler; lower cost

47 (a) disk/files

Exercise 8

48 D

49 (it is) static//can be reviewed

50 C

51 U

52 C

53 anticipating//recognizing

54 discourse structure

55 topic sentence

56 H//J

57 E

58 L

59 C

60 G

61 D

62 B

63 I

64 G

65 E

66 functional

67 junior to middle

68 advertise/(through) advertisement/ short list

69 directed/direct approach/headhunting

70 T

71 ?

72 certain disciplines

73 useful/important/tool

74 D

75 C

76 5

Writing

Exercise 1

Title	Topic	Question
1	Solar radiation	How can it provide domestic hot water and lighting?
2	Inner four planets of the solar system	What are they like?
3	Beetle	What is its life cycle?
4	Unemployment trends in the UK over the four years	What happened?
5	Tourist arrivals in Cyprus	How did they change between 1977 and 1988?

Exercise 3

1 collection/conversion

2 storage

3 distribution/output

Title	Topic	Question
6	The changes modern high technology is making to the way we work	Is it of benefit to all of society?
7	The rights which higher mammals have*	Do higher mammals have rights?* Should they be used in laboratory experiments?
8	The increasing number of young people studying and working overseas	Will this help to bring about greater international co-operation?

Note that there are two possible ways of interpreting title 6: **either** *you may treat the statement that animals have rights as a* **fact**, *in which case it is not the question. Or you could treat it as subjective view, in which case you would focus on it.*

Exercise 12

Modern technology can transform all of society. For example, a great deal more is produced on a farm with the aid of modern technology than the yields which are achieved without such help. It is therefore clear that it provides benefit for us. Some countries in the Third World, however, do not have access to the latest technology and cannot keep pace with those that do.

Exercise 13

1   Selecting material

No reference is made to whether or not animals do, or should, have rights (see exercise 9); otherwise selection of material is good.

2   Organizing your ideas clearly and logically

The first paragraph is the argument for laboratory experiments, the second is against and the last is the writer's opinion and conclusion. The essay is organized but none of this is made clear. The writer should have made the order clear for the reader. Note also that there is a logical inconsistency in the argument: it is because monkeys are so similar to humans that they are used for experiments (see the last sentence).

Relevant examples are given. Can you think of others?

The answer makes good use of linking expressions.

3   Using correct forms

Check thoroughly. There are many errors in grammar and spelling. Check the use of prepositions and articles, for instance.

There are also many examples of inappropriate language use.

The language is too emotional and there are too many contractions (This's, lab., etc.) instead of full forms.

Listening

Exercise 1

Questions 1–4

You cannot anticipate the exact content but you do know:

● that somebody called Abdul is being given directions;

● that he is travelling by train;

● that he will then go by underground (so he is going to a city);

● that he is meeting one or two people.

Questions 5–10

This is an example of a form-filling exercise where it is very easy to anticipate the type of information needed:

● somebody (probably Abdul) is filling in a form at the college badminton club; he is probably applying to join the club.

Exercise 2

1 directions;

2 trains: times, destinations, direct or stopping at all stations;

3 underground lines, destination;

4 description of people: number, sex, clothing;

5 name;

6 subject (probably a science subject – see faculty);

7 number (no. is an abbreviation for 'number');

8 address;

9 level or standard;

10 number.

Listening exercises

Discussion comes before the answers in each section.

Section 1

You have an explanation on the tape for the example. You may often have to deduce things from information given, rather than being given the exact answer. You must listen for **information** rather than for specific words.

For **question 4** the speaker said she would be with Tom and they would both be carrying sports gear. **Questions 5 and 7** test letters and numbers and must be answered correctly.

Question 6: spelling of 'electronics' is not important.

Question 8: the '36D' (or '36d') must be accurate but the spelling is not important for 'Spring Court'.

Questions 9 and 10: again you must deduce these as the exact answer is not given on the tape.

1 C

2 B

3 B

4 D

5 Amin

6 electronics

7 92 YG 30 44

8 36D Spring Court

9 average

10 3–5

Section 2

Question 11: the key phrase was 'two main sections … and another … '

Question 12: there are two categories – general loan and reference. Non-reference books are therefore general loan. But some coursebooks are on twenty-four-hour loan.

Question 13 and 14 are a kind of table gap-filling exercise. Biblitas 'has the advantage of having a separate subject index'.

Question 15 is a picture type answer, as in question 1. The centre is 'across the corridor directly opposite the reference section … '

Question 16: you can anticipate from the question that there will be a description of the equipment available. 'All … with the exception of the computer monitors … ' and 'this applies also to the two television receivers … ' give you the answer.

Note the importance of reading ahead: If you do not have the answer to question 16 by the time you hear ' … the two television receivers … ', leave it and concentrate on question 17 which also refers to satellite television. If you worry about question 16 you may miss both answers.

Question 18: should be straightforward. You know you are listening for a time; common sense tells you 'three' is afternoon, not night.

Question, 19: the important phrase in the question is 'In total': this includes English. This should remind you how important it is to read the question carefully.

Question 20: we are told the sessions are on the 'first and third Thursday of each month', i.e. 2 and 16. We do not know about 30.

11 3

12 no

13 all

14 author and title

15

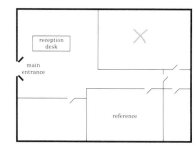

16 A B C and D

17 D

18 no

19 6

20 (Thursday) 2 and 16

These questions are perhaps the most difficult in IELTS. You only have to give a short answer but it is important to know what the question is asking. It is important to read the questions quickly and to identify the key words in order to know what to listen for.

Sometimes, in the multiple-choice, for example, you will not be able to make an instant decision. If necessary you can make a note on a particular question in your own language while you listen. You can then come back to it in the time you are given to check your answers.

Question 21: the tape says 'course'; the question says 'year'; the key word is 'foundation'.

Question 22: the tutor begins to list the options: you can anticipate the answer is coming.

Question 23: she is already interested in writing computer games; 'I'd like to … ' means that she hopes to do it. Keep your answer short. It asks for a phrase; you do not have to write a sentence.

Question 24: the tutor says: 'No, I see that'. This is agreeing with a negative idea. 'Go on' means 'continue'. This may be an example where you might have to make a note and come back to the question at the end of the session.

Question 25: again the tutor says 'no' but it is not a rejection. In fact, the excellent facilities are described as encouragement and 'you'll enjoy that' is added.

Questions 26–28: this type of question is quite common but the exact form of answer varies. Again, make a note in a way that is clear to you, if necessary, and make sure you have followed the instructions exactly when you check at the end of the section.

Question 26: we know writing is a problem; there is no information about reading.

Question 27: the tutor suggests both EFL and study skills classes.

Question 28: 'starting … next year' means 'delaying … for one year'. If you are not sure of the word 'delaying' then guess.

Questions 29 and 30: there are no restrictions here. It is in your interests to use the minimum number of words in order to save time. You must have 'telephone'.

21 6 modules/options

22 art and design

23 (produce) educational software/games

24 B

25 C

26 N

27 A

28 A

29 (by) telephone

30 visit/in person

Questions 31–35 are examples of a gapped summary (see the reading section if you need to remind yourself about this question type). You must therefore expect the wording to be slightly different from the actual words used on the tape. During the time you are given to read the questions quickly survey the summary or notes to find out what the topic is (the recording helps you here) and then focus on the gaps and the words and headings before and after them. Note that there are no restrictions on the number of words you can use – but a word or short phrase is all that is needed.

Question 31: the speaker uses 'you' but is clearly talking about students. You could use 'as equals' from the recording or you could use another word, such as 'equally', but keep the answer short.

Question 32: none of the words here is exactly as on the recording but you should be ready for the answer as you hear another key word: 'independent'. Then you should recognize 'working(ing) out' even if you do not know what it means. The spelling of programme is not important (plan or timetable would be acceptable also).

Question 33: the word 'different' should alert you to the answer.

Question 34: you may not know the words 'structure' or 'discourse' but the speaker explains what they mean. 'Pronunciation' gives you the signal to focus your listening.

Question 35: you may be tempted to write 'a particular topic' but we 'take part' in seminars, not topics.

Note that you are not told to go on to questions 36–38. You must be ready to switch from the summary to a completely different type of question. This is why a survey of all the questions is so important. You must be prepared for the next one or two questions and not just the one you are trying to answer at the time. Note also that you often need to use specific information to work out an answer to a more general question. As you work through the sections of the subtest you will probably find that the questions become more general and that you need a wider range of specific information to answer them.

Question 36: the lecturer talks about linking but does not give an explicit example of link words.

Question 37: the speaker is talking about 'today …

Question 38: it would be sensible for the lecturer to do this but from the information in the recording we cannot tell.

31 (more) as equals/equally

32 study programme/plan

33 tutorials

34 structure discourse/organize what they say

35 (a) seminar(s)

36 F

37 F

38 ?

Section two: further practice

Paper 1

1 C

2 C

3 C

4 I

5 B

6 H

7 A

8 D

9 find confidence

10 cautious//reluctant [*reluctant to move* is wrong – too many words]

11 (stable) core

12 (personnel) recruitment/management [*personnel recruitment and management* is wrong – too many words]

13 implement/build strategies // structure themselves

14 B

15 passport to modern life; precondition of national prosperity

16 C

17 I

18 D

19 G

20 C

21 E

22 C

23 C

24 B

25 B

26 II

27 F

28 T

29 need

30 legislation

31 resources

32 environmental audits

33 independent

34 assessed

35 I [*many*, not *all*]

36 I [*proposes*, not *insists*]

37 NC [*on* means *about*, not *at*]

38 public attitude; insurance markets; national legislation

39 systematic; periodic; documented; objective (evaluation)

40 ii

Paper 2

1 personnel

2 (large) multinationals

3 standards of competence

4 formal recognition

5 multidisciplinary

6 centres of excellence

7 flexible, modular

8 code of practice

9 the importance of

10 motivation, training and leadership

11 business awareness

12 external communications

13 management skills

14 strategic vision

15 false[although *some* may]

16 false [future aim]

17 overrated (potential) demand

18 speed (up) decision-making

19 to cut costs//cost cutting//cutting costs

[Note: answers 18 and 19 can be in either order]

20 C

21 A

22 C

23 B

24 A

25 K

26 H

27 G

28 L

29 I

30 partial success

31 3 [*three* is wrong]

32 a/one fifth // 1/5 // 20%

33 D

34 A

35 C

36 C

37 A

38 U

39 D

40 U

Paper 3

1 C

2 G

3 B

4 H

5 J

6 A

7 SFS

8 S

9 N

10 SFS

11 S

12 N

13 NCG

14 T

15 F

16 F

17 best-selling periodicals

18 the educational establishment

19 inferior cultural form

20 various disenfranchised groups

21 of academic courses

[Note: answers 17–21 **must** have **three words** each]

22 B [evidence is number of specialist shops, mainstream bookshops stocking comics, number of publishers, attendance at comics conventions; collecting comics and adult readership are not evidence]

23 B [one comic only in survey]

24 D [*considered*, not *proved*]

25 D

26 their potential // potential use

27 have value

28 C

29 B

30 A

31 B

32 C

33 B

34 C

35 hardest to//most difficult to

36 (desperately) overcrowded slums//squatter settlements//(apparently)hopeless slums// overcrowded conditions//makeshift hovels

37 (significant) improvement//government help//adequate infrastructure

38 constricting economic development//depleting rural resources

39 continue to//choose to//elect to

40 likely to continue//unlikely to change//inevitable

Paper 4

1 B//I

2 B//I

[Note: answers 1 and 2 can be either way round]

3 F

4 C//H//L

5 C//H//L

[Note: answers 4 and 5 can be any two of the letters given, in any order]

6 manufactured goods and

7 aid stagnated and

8 one or two

9 scarce foreign exchange

10 recession and slow

11 whole range of//range of new

12 could earn more

13 home markets and

14 tariffs and other

15 Third World products

16 numeracy//accounts

17 (basic) economics//economic affairs

18 management (skills)/(training)

19 technical knowledge//(specialist) skills/understanding

[Note: answers 16–19 can be in any order]

20 T

21 F

22 E

23 A

24 B

25 J

26 F

27 personal skills//co-operation

28 balancing skills//communication

[Note: answers 27 and 28 can be either way round]

29 B

30 3 [building personal skills; courage to take risks; ability to cope with uncertainty]

31 F [text states *liable to be*]

32 NC [text states *may*, not *will*]

33 T

34 NC [*criminal*, yes; *civil* not stated]

35 T

36 (an) environmental audit

37 warranties//indemnity

38 warranties//indemnity

[Note: answers 37 and 38 can be either way round]

39 enforcing security

40 (on) termination (of the lease)

The British Council publishes a number of titles in English Language Teaching and the growing field of British Studies, both independently and in collaboration with other publishers.

Areas covered include:

- examinations
- British Studies
- Business English
- teacher education
- self-access
- information resources
- journals

If you would like a copy of the British Council ELT and British Studies catalogue, or want to order any of our publications, contact your local British Council office, or:

Keltic International
39 Alexandra Road
Addlestone
Surrey KT15 2PQ
Telephone (01932) 854776
Fax (01932) 849528

If you would like to receive information about future British Council ELT and British Studies publications, please fill in the form below and return it to:

British Studies and Publications
Consultancy Group
The British Council
Medlock Street
Manchester M15 4AA

Name ....
....

Institution ....
....

Address ....
....
....

Special interests

General English ☐

Business English ☐

Teacher education ☐

Self-access ☐

British studies ☐

(please tick one or more boxes)